BBC Books, an imprint of Ebury Publishing
20 Vauxhall Bridge Road
London SW1V 2SA

BBC Books is part of the Penguin Random House group of companies whose addresses can
be found at global.penguinrandomhouse.com

Penguin
Random House
UK

This book is published to accompany the television series *Strictly Come Dancing*,
first broadcast on BBC One in 2023

Executive Producer: Sarah James
Series Director: Nikki Parsons
Series Producer: Nicola Fitzgerald
Series Editors: Jack Gledhill and Robin Lee-Perrella

With thanks to: Eve Winstanley, Harriet Frost, Clemmie Kirby, Sophie Hoyles,
Kate Lawson and Victoria Dalton.

First published by BBC Books in 2023
www.penguin.co.uk
A CIP catalogue record for this book is available from the British Library
ISBN 9781785948534

Printed and bound in Italy by Elcograf S.p.A.
The authorised representative in the EEA is Penguin Random House Ireland, Morrison Chambers,
32 Nassau Street, Dublin D02 YH68.

MIX
Paper from
responsible sources
FSC® C018179

Picture Credits: © BBC Archive. BBC/Ray Burmiston: pp. 7, 12, 14, 16, 18, 20, 22, 29, 30, 32, 34, 36, 40, 42,
44, 46, 50, 52, 54, 56, 62, 64, 71, 75, 76, 78, 82, 84, 87, 92, 94, 96, 98, 101, 104, 106, 113, 114, 116, 119,
121, 122, 124. BBC/Guy Levy: pp. 9, 10, 11, 24, 25, 26, 27, 48, 59, 60, 61, 67, 68, 102, 103, 105, 111.
BBC/Kieron McCarron: p. 49. BBC/David Venni: p. 100.

2024

ANNUAL

Contents

Meet the
Pro Dancers

Fun &
Trivia

Head judge Shirley started off the series with a twirl, taking to the floor with her fellow judges on the launch show, and she says she always loves putting her dancing shoes on for a *Strictly* routine. But once she's off her feet and in her seat, the Queen of Latin is focused on the class of '23 – and she likes what she sees.

'This year's line-up is probably the best we've had so far,' she says. 'Whatever people may lack in dance experience, they'll certainly make up for in larger-than-life personalities. There's a wide range of ages, which is fabulous, and everybody already seems to have blended in together and become a family. The launch show was absolutely spectacular and I loved meeting all the new celebrities, who are hilarious. I'm very excited for this series.'

The former Latin champ, who has a 40-year career in both competing and teaching, was thrilled by last year's Grand Final and believes all four contestants – Fleur East, Helen Skelton, Molly Rainford and winner Hamza Yassin – could have been crowned champion.

'The Glitterball trophy could have gone to anybody who was in the Final because they were all amazing, with inspiring journeys,' she says. 'I always have faith that the public will pick out the person that they feel warranted it throughout the series, so Hamza was a very worthy champion.

'The most memorable moment for me has to be Hamza's Salsa, in week four, which caught us all by surprise. He lifted Jowita and threw her all over the place. So he not only had great timing and strength, but he was also extremely humble, and he danced everything from his heart.

'It was a great Final and I think we're heading towards another phenomenal Final this year.'

Presiding over the judges' panel since 2017, Shirley has the measure of what makes a *Strictly* champ, and the qualities they need to get to the Grand Final.

'First of all, you have to have an ear for music, and that goes without saying,' she says. 'Music has to come into your ear and out through your body. Coordination will help, although you can learn that, but if you can't feel and count music, you're in trouble. Then you have to go into this with the heart of a lion, a strong work ethic, great listening skills and not be frightened to ask questions. Then it is practice. So even before you get to technique, creativity and choreography, you need all these things.'

As a judge, Shirley has an eagle eye for detail, but she's also looking for enthusiasm.

'I want a little bit of technique, I want a little bit of leg action, a little bit of flexibility, a little bit of coordination,' she says. 'Posture and musicality are high on my list. However, at the end of the day, if somebody lacks a bit in technique but brings that heart and soul to the dance, and I can see they are really trying, that also goes down well in my book.

'I'm known as a technician and in the first five weeks I like to make sure that they've got some technical fundamentals under their belt. From there, we're looking for the creativity and everything else.'

Looking forward to the new series, Shirley says she can't choose her favourite week, because she loves them all.

'I love Halloween Week because I love dressing up. I love going to Blackpool because that's like going home. I like Musicals Week, I love the Christmas show and I love the Grand Final – and all the weeks in between are just as exciting.

'The hardest part for me will be sending anybody home at all. So I have a plea for the audience: If you want someone to stay in, please vote!'

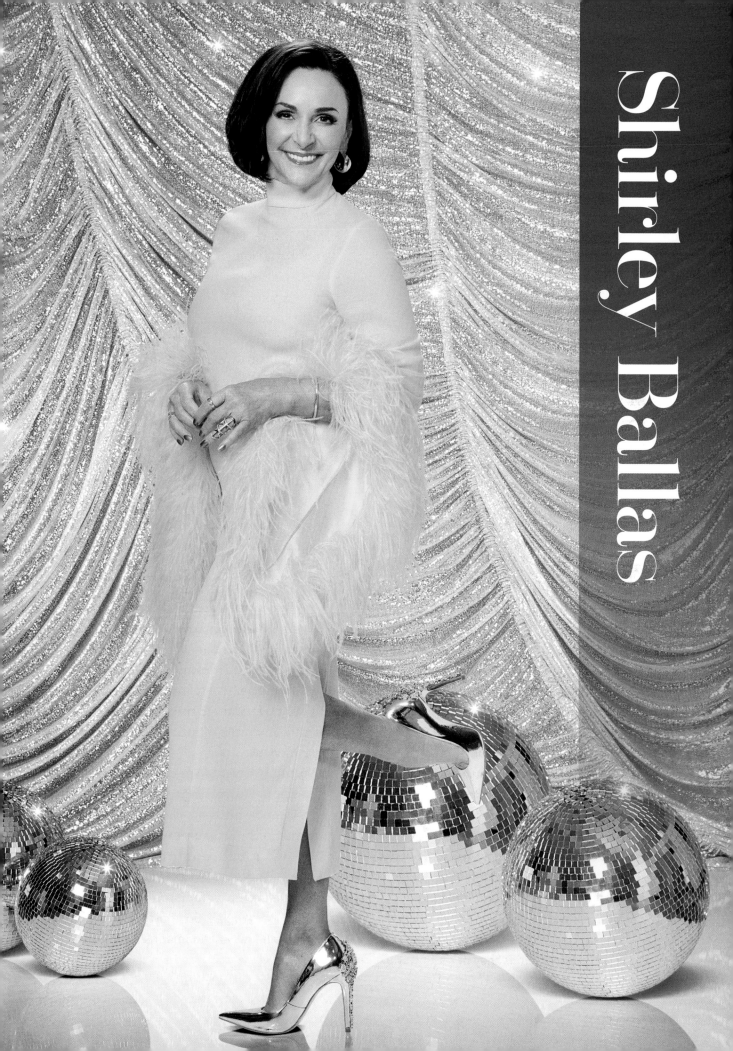

Shirley Ballas

Hamza Yassin

Winner's story

Hamza Yassin unleashed his wild side on the *Strictly* dance floor and found that dancing was second nature to him. But the wildlife cameraman and presenter, who won series 20 with pro dance partner Jowita Przystał, is still stunned to have been crowned *Strictly Come Dancing* champ.

'Words can't describe the feeling of lifting that Glitterball trophy,' he says. 'I never thought in a million years that we were going to win. I was speechless. You could see how much emotion ran through both me and Jowita. It was fantastic.

'*Strictly* is one of the best things I've ever done in my life, and I couldn't have done it without Jowita.'

Hamza, who was born in Sudan and moved to the UK with his family when he was eight, starred in CBBC's *Let's Go for a Walk*, as Ranger Hamza. Now living in the Highlands of Scotland, he fronted the Channel 4 documentary *Scotland: My Life in the Wild* and the four-part series *Escape to the Wilderness*. It was there that he

also discovered his love of Scottish ceilidhs and, although he never considered himself a good dancer, he jumped at the chance to try his luck on the show.

'As soon as I heard the word *Strictly* I said, "I'm in!"' he says. 'I love dancing. I wouldn't have said I was a dancer at the beginning of this, and I still wouldn't now, but I know how to dance those particular dances. It's amazing how two people can move an audience with a dance. Physically and mentally, it was an amazing experience.'

Hamza kicked off his *Strictly* journey with an impressive Foxtrot, earning him joint first place at the top of the leader board with Will Mellor, but he admits he had a few jitters before his first dance.

'I've faced polar bears, I've faced lions that are not happy with me and crocodiles that want to bite me in half, but nothing beats hearing Alan Dedicoat's famous voice saying, "Dancing the Foxtrot, Hamza Yassin and Jowita Przystał." That's when the nerves kick in. But Jowita had an

amazing knack of calming me down, and she'd say, "It's just me, you and the music. It's just what we did in training. Let's go out there and do it again."

'I was out of my comfort zone, but it was a good challenge for me and I pushed myself. All I wanted to do was to keep Jowita happy. At the end of the day, if she was smiling, I'd done my job. If the judges' comments were good, that was a bonus.'

The fleet-footed presenter says he fell for the ballroom dances and loved both the week-one Foxtrot and his amazing American Smooth, which earned him two perfect 10s in Blackpool. The pair's African-themed Couple's Choice also holds a special place in his heart.

'I am a ballroom boy, for sure,' he says. 'In the Latin dances you can be freer, but ballroom is either right or wrong, and there's no in between. I fell in love with the Foxtrot, so when

it came up again as American Smooth Foxtrot, with lifts, and we danced it in Blackpool wearing the tail suits, I was in heaven.

'For the Couple's Choice, I wanted to do something that represents my three mothers: Mother Africa, Mother Nature and my mother. The choreographer was from West Africa, the costume was from East Africa and the song was from South Africa. It meant the world to me, and I cried at the end of it. I loved Motsi's comment to Jowita, that she needed to get a DNA test to prove she's not African.'

Years of carrying heavy camera equipment and tossing the caber in Highland Games means Hamza's upper-body strength is exceptional, which he demonstrated by dead-lifting Jowita above his head in his week-four Salsa. The pair earned 39 points for the daring routine, which was also a crowd-pleaser on the Live Tour.

'On day one of rehearsals, Jowita asked me

to lift her, then she uttered a phrase that will stay with me forever, saying, "I feel comfortable in your arms when you lift me." As the lifter, knowing your partner trusts you 100 per cent is crucial.'

Hamza is full of praise for his professional partner and says she always got the best out of him.

'You can't expect to go into *Strictly* half-heartedly and win it, and Jowita knew I wanted to be the best I could be so she pushed me as far as I could go,' he says. 'It was a beautiful journey, and I learned a lot about my own limits. When I said, "I can't do any more," Jowita could get another 75 per cent out of that tank. She is the best teacher and went above and beyond to make sure that I was comfortable in each dance. She has changed my life.'

Usually found crawling in the undergrowth, looking for the wonders of the natural world, Hamza enjoyed getting glammed up.

'I'm usually in camouflage jackets and long boots and covered in ticks and mud,' he says. 'So it was an absolute privilege to be dressed by the world's best costume designers, having everything tailor-made for me and having my hair done. I felt properly pampered, and I loved going out there knowing I looked fan-dabi-dozi.'

The TV star says he has gained so much more than dance skills on his journey.

'*Strictly* has opened the eyes of the public to who I am and what my mission is, which is to look after this natural world,' he says. 'I have fallen in love with dance and the joy that it brings to people's faces. I gained fitness while doing something I loved.

'Most of all I take away the friendship with Jowita, the camaraderie with all my celebrity friends and the conviction that if you can dream it, you can do it.'

Angela Scanlon

Presenter Angela is swapping her iconic *Robot Wars* jumpsuit for a splash of *Strictly* sparkle and says she's 'secretly thrilled about the prospect of all that glitter'.

'In theory, I love the idea of being *Strictly*-fied, but I'm quite a tomboy, so I'm usually either in jeans and a jumper or I'm in a tall skirt and a sweater,' she says. 'But I'm up for it. I'm going to surrender to it all!'

She is relishing the challenge of learning Latin and ballroom and is 'so happy' to be paired with series-20 finalist Carlos Gu for the experience.

'I haven't stepped outside of my comfort zone for a long time and I'm ready to be properly challenged,' she says. 'And how lucky I am to get to do something where I'm being physically challenged by the best teachers in the world. It feels like an indulgence in one way, so I'm very excited.'

Born in County Meath, Ireland, Angela began her career as a stylist and fashion journalist before moving into fashion TV. She has fronted various documentaries and in 2016 became co-host of *Robot Wars* alongside Dara Ó Briain. She went on to host interior design show *Your Home Made Perfect* on the BBC and has her own Saturday-night chat show, *Angela Scanlon's Ask Me Anything* on RTÉ.

Angela says her signature dance move is 'the running man' and her previous dance experience was a very different style to the *Strictly* dances.

'I did Irish dancing when I was younger, where you're expressly told to remain stiff as a board from the waist up, so I'm not sure how that's going to go down in Latin or in ballroom!'

The Irish presenter is raring to go on all the Latin and ballroom disciplines but is particularly keen on two very different styles of dance.

'They're opposite ends of the spectrum, but I really love the Charleston and the Rumba,' she says. 'I don't know how I'm going to deal with the Charleston, physically, because it feels very energetic and I'm not great on a trampoline, so I feel like I'll be tested in more ways than one. The Rumba may also be a challenge, because I play the joker quite well but anything that's very slow and intense gives me the heebie-jeebies.'

While she is keen to get as far as she can in the show, Angela says she hasn't been eyeing up the opposition.

'When we were in training for our first group dance, I was just intent on getting my feet to make the right moves, never mind looking around to what everybody else is doing,' she laughs. 'I'm very much trying to get control of my own limbs, so I don't know that I've had time to scope out the competition.

'I don't yet have my eye on the prize because I'm trying to be involved in the process, not the outcome. But I'd love to get to Blackpool because I believe the dance floor is bouncy and I like the sound of that.'

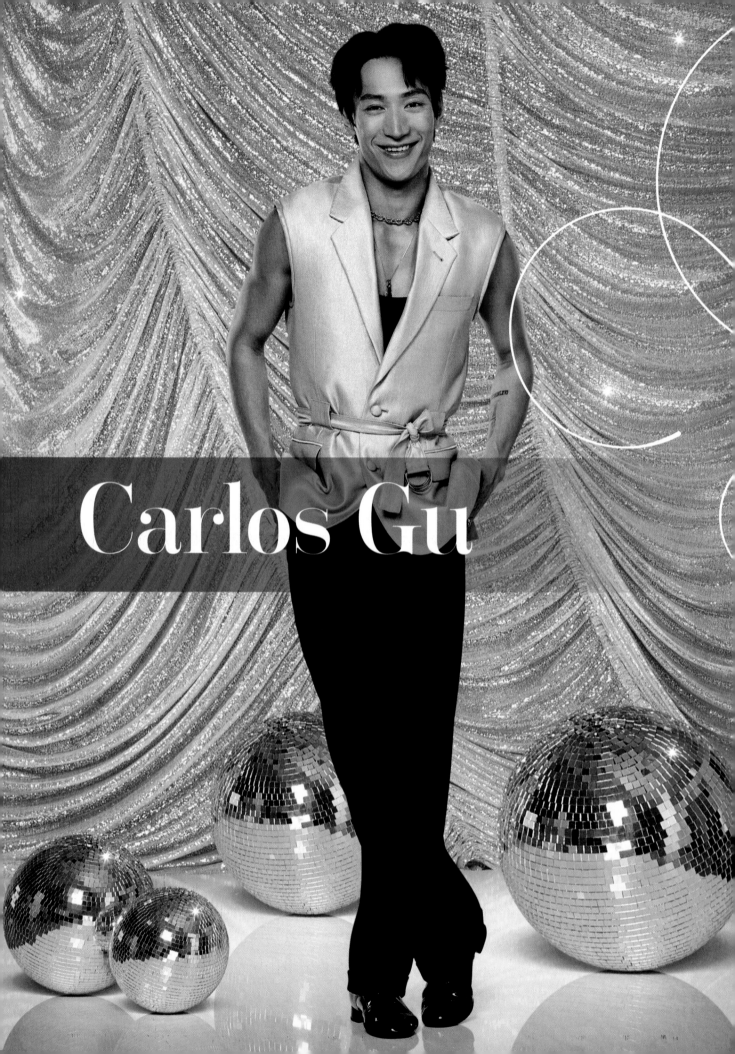

Carlos Gu

In his first year on the show, Carlos danced his way to the Final with singer and actress Molly Rainford. For this series, he is taking to the floor with presenter Angela Scanlon, and he is hoping to make it all the way to the Final again – if they can stop laughing long enough to train.

'We're having so much fun together and we laugh all the time,' he says. 'From the second we met it's been great, and by the first week we were laughing so hard we were literally crying.

'Angela has rhythm in her body but she doesn't know it's there at the moment,' he says. 'It's my job to bring it out and help her use that tool. But her strength may be her warm, positive energy and her smile, which makes everyone around her want to smile too.'

Angela grew up practising Irish dancing, which requires a straight back and fast feet, but Carlos insists that's unlikely to help her when it comes to Strictly.

'Latin and ballroom are completely different,' he says. 'You have to dance with a partner; the technique is different and is very specific. So anybody who has dance experience but not ballroom experience still has to start from scratch. Being a singer will help with rhythm, being an actor will help the performance, but in terms of dance, everyone has to start from the beginning.'

Born in Taiyuan, China, Carlos started dancing at 11 and studied dance at Tianjin University of Sport and the Beijing Dance Academy. At 14, he competed at the German Open Championships, coming third, and went on to become Chinese National Latin Champion. Making his Strictly debut last year, he got tantalisingly close to the Glitterball trophy and says he made a friend for life in Molly.

'Before we started, I could absolutely not imagine myself stepping into the Final in my first year,' he says. 'I knew I would do my best to help my partner to dance and get the best out of them. But Molly worked hard and improved so much. The energy between us was amazing and we really encouraged each other. Molly is like a little sister to me. We had such a great time'.

Carlos says Molly picked up routines quickly and wowed him in week two with her Quickstep.

'She was so good at the Quickstep, but my favourite dance was the Rumba, which was amazing.'

Carlos says the first year on the show taught him 'resilience and to be open and accepting of your partner's potential and help them obtain it.'

Now settled in, he can't wait to take to the dance floor for a second year.

'Last year there was a lot to learn because I'd watched the show on television but had no idea what's behind the scenes,' he says. 'I'm even more excited this year because I know what to expect. Being paired with Angela is another bonus because she has a great vibe and she works hard. I just want to give her the best, most enjoyable and most memorable journey possible.'

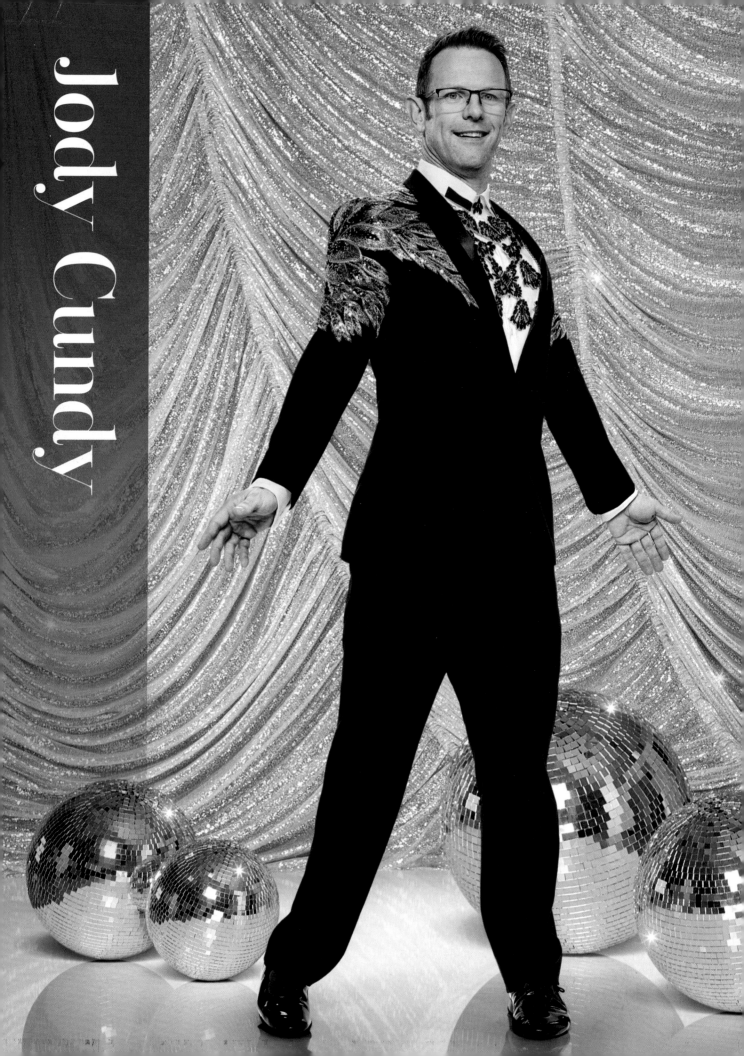

Jody Cundy

With eight Paralympic golds and 23 world titles, Jody's trophy cabinet is already well stocked. Now hoping to add the *Strictly* Glitterball trophy to his haul, he admits he is starting with 'zero' dancing skills.

'My dance experience is absolutely non-existent,' he laughs. 'My best dance move is moving away from the dance floor when anybody's coming to pull me on. Getting on the iconic *Strictly* dance floor, by choice, is going be an experience and a half.'

Born in Cambridgeshire, Jody had his limb amputated below the knee at three and was given a prosthetic leg. At eight, he discovered swimming and went on to represent Britain at the Paralympics three times, from 1996, winning three golds and two bronze medals. In 2006, he switched to cycling, winning gold on his debut at the World Championships that year. He went on to win five more golds at the Paralympics as well as breaking the world record in the 1km Time Trial and becoming the first British male athlete to win medals at seven consecutive Paralympic Games.

As a sports star, Jody, who is paired with reigning champ Jowita Przystał, is at peak fitness and believes being used to training hard could help in the rehearsal room.

'Obviously, in both swimming and cycling, we train for hours on end, so hopefully that helps,' he says. For me, it's about being taught all of the things that I need to be taught and trying to take on as much as I can and turn that into something that resembles dance.'

After Jody's success in the pool and on the track, *Strictly* represents a whole new challenge – and one he is embracing wholeheartedly.

'I have confidence in riding a bike, and I know exactly what I'm doing there, but when it comes to something that I don't know I tend to shy away,' he says. 'But when I got the call asking me to do this I thought, "This is cool and not many people get asked to do it." I need to get out there and say, "Actually, I can do this, and I can do it on a big stage, where we have professional dancers teaching us how to do it properly." What better place to learn? Yes, there are going to be millions of people watching me stand all over my dance partner's feet, but hopefully they can watch me go on a journey from zero to lifting up a trophy at the end!

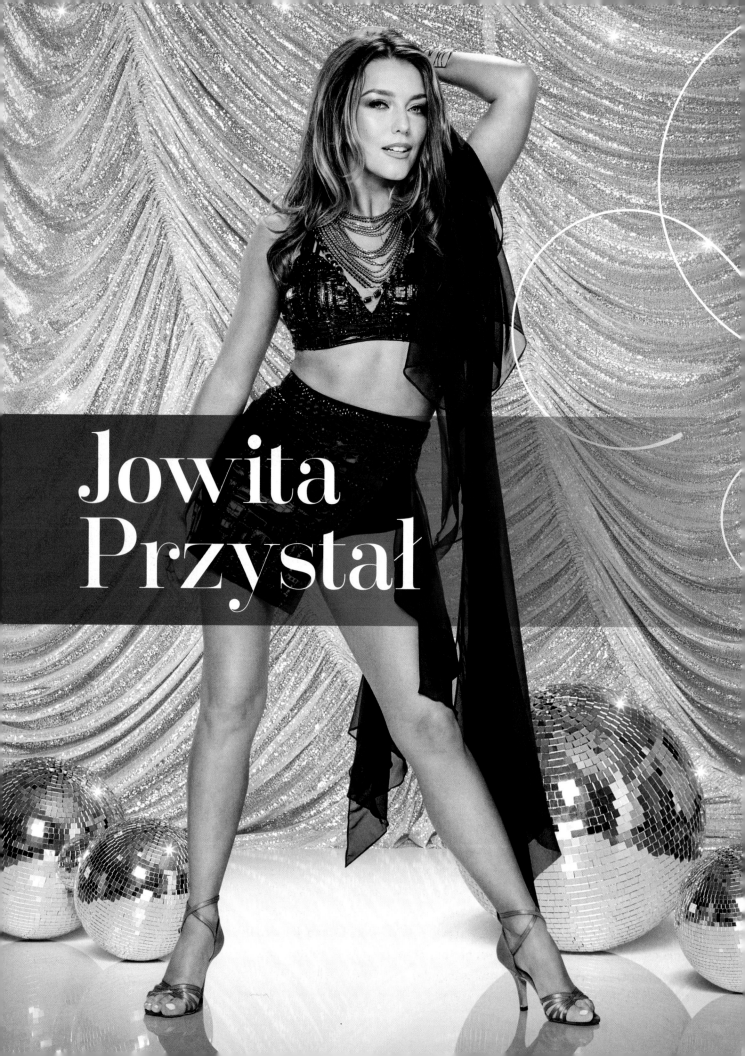

Jowita
Przystał

Reigning champ Jowita swept to victory in her first year paired with a celebrity, bagging the Glitterball trophy with wildlife filmmaker Hamza Yassin last year. Now she is back in the saddle with Paralympian cyclist Jody Cundy and is hoping to get on track for another Final.

'Jody is the sweetest man, so generous and kind, and I adore him already,' she says. 'I'm honoured to be able to guide him through this process because he's a living legend, with 23 titles. He won his first medal in 1994, the year I was born.

'His mentality is so strong. He is an athlete so we are on the same page in many ways. I'm so happy to work with him. He's a trooper.'

Jody has Paralympic golds in both swimming and cycling, and Jowita says that's a good sign. 'Everything is possible,' she says. 'He went from swimming to cycling so he can go from cycling to dancing. I just need him to stop overthinking.'

Jowita has nothing but admiration for Jody's attitude.

'He's a fighter and he won't give up,' she says. If a step is difficult for him and I say I'll work something different out, he'll say, "No, I want to do it." It's beautiful to see somebody who's so committed.

'My job is to make him as comfortable as I can in the dance and to be the best version of myself, so he gets the full experience of Strictly.'

Jowita started dancing at six, in her native Poland, and moved into ballroom and Latin at 12. She went on to become Polish Open Latin Champion. She made her first appearance on Strictly in 2020, after winning The Greatest Dancer with Michael Danilczuk, and the following year she joined the pro dance team. Lifting the trophy last year was an emotional moment.

'It meant everything to me to see the Glitterball trophy in Hamza's hands, and I couldn't be prouder of him,' she says. 'Going into the Final, it wasn't about winning because getting him there was everything I could wish for. I just wanted him to be happy and proud of himself, so winning was just the cherry on the top of everything.

'It taught me that if you work really hard and you really want to achieve your goal, anything is possible. Hamza went from literally not knowing how to do a single dance move and, in the end, he became a dancer. I'm proud that I could be by his side throughout his journey.

'The other thing last year taught me is that I need a lot of coffee!'

This year, Jowita kicked off the series by reuniting with Hamza for a final dance on the Strictly dance floor, recreating their incredible Salsa for the launch show.

'I'm not someone who usually cries a lot, but I couldn't hold back the tears,' she says. 'Throughout the competition there are a lot of things to think about, but during this last dance, nothing else mattered. It was just the two of us on the dance floor, and he's such a good dancer now, it felt like I was dancing with a professional. It was amazing.'

Jody is starting his Strictly journey from scratch, with no dance experience, but Jowita sees his potential.

'Jody is very shy and he doesn't dance at all. He literally hides rather than dances at a party,' she says. 'But, after Strictly, this will never happen again. My goal is to make him a dancer and, for me, if he can take his fiancée, Lucy, out and ask her for a dance, that will be my Strictly Glitterball trophy.'

Amanda Abbington

Actress Amanda will be showing off her competitive streak when she takes to the *Strictly* dance floor, and she is over the moon to be dancing on the show.

'I'm thrilled to have been asked to do *Strictly*. I'm actually really shy and self-conscious, so this will be a great opportunity for me to overcome that,' she says. 'Plus, I get to learn to dance, which I am incredibly excited about. I'm really looking forward to the training, too – I'm quite competitive, as my family and friends will tell you.'

The *Sherlock* star jumped at the chance to glam up and throw herself into the routines, and she is keen to show that age is no barrier to being fab-u-lous.

'I don't like the idea of women becoming invisible at a certain age, so I'm going to stand up for the 50-plus women and go and have a little dance for them,' she says. 'I also said yes to embarrass my two teenagers. Actually, they want to come to the live shows, but not to support me – they're huge fans of Zara McDermott!'

Growing up in Hertfordshire, Amanda was encouraged by a teacher to take up acting and was snapped up by an agent before she'd left her local drama school. She went on to star in *Dream Team*, the comedy series *Man Stroke Woman* and *After You've Gone* with Nicholas Lyndhurst. In 2013, she landed the role of department head Miss Mardle in the period drama *Mr Selfridge*, and the following year she joined Benedict Cumberbatch and Martin Freeman in the hit drama *Sherlock*, playing Mary Morstan, Dr Watson's wife and a former assassin. She boasts an extensive theatre résumé, including Florian Zeller's drama *The Son*, Steven Moffat's *The Unfriend* and the Yasmina Reza four-hander *God of Carnage*.

Paired with Giovanni Pernice for the show, Amanda says she is ready to put in the work to make her routines as slick as possible.

'I need a lot of discipline and I'm a bit of a perfectionist, so I have to keep going over something until I'm happy. But the most important requirement from my partner is a sense of humour because if you're in a room with somebody for six or seven hours a day, your sense of humour needs to click.'

Although she says she was 'treading on a lot of people's toes' in the first group rehearsals, she is hoping some of her acting skills will stand her in good stead for perfecting her ballroom and Latin moves.

'I know rhythm and I can pick things up quickly when I'm learning lines, which feels like a similar learning method to memorising steps,' she says. 'But getting the character is important, too!'

Giovanni Pernice

Former champ Giovanni is paired with *Sherlock* star Amanda Abbington and is hoping ballroom and Latin steps will prove 'elementary' to the award-winning actress.

'I am very happy to be partnering Amanda,' he says. 'She has a lot of potential. We also got along very well, very quickly. She's lovely to talk to and she has rhythm and movement. It has to be polished, but it's in there. We just have to bring it out. I'm genuinely excited to see what she's going to bring to the table.'

The Italian pro dancer says Amanda was over the moon to be paired with him when they met at 221B Baker Street, the fictional home of Sherlock Holmes. 'She screamed,' he says. 'I've never heard anything like this before. She was very, very happy, which is a lovely reaction to see.'

While Amanda's acting skills may help her get into character for the dances, Giovanni says the footwork and technique come first.

'Basically, as with all the celebrities, it's a new language and a completely new thing for them to do. So the acting and performing will be there at some point, but at the beginning, it's all about learning the dance, learning the technique, learning the steps. The acting is the cherry on the cake.'

Sicilian Giovanni decided to become a dancer after watching the UK TV show *Come Dancing*. He left home at 14 to study dance in Bologna, and in 2012 he was crowned Italian champion, going on to compete in numerous international contests and coming second in the International Open Latin in Slovenia in 2014. A year later,

he joined *Strictly* and has since reached the Grand Final with Georgia May Foote, Debbie McGee and Faye Tozer, before finally lifting the Glitterball trophy with Rose Ayling-Ellis in series 19. Last year, he partnered Radio 2 presenter Richie Anderson but was eliminated in week three.

'Richie is a very kind person and we had a great laugh together. I've been lucky over the years with all my partners and I'm friends with pretty much all of them.'

Having lifted the trophy himself, Giovanni says one quality is necessary above all others if you want to be a *Strictly* champ.

'Commitment is the most important thing,' he says. 'If you have commitment, then you're halfway there.'

Giovanni keeps his Glitterball trophy in pride of place in his living room, next to the Must-See Moment BAFTA he won for his powerful Couple's Choice dance with Rose Ayling-Ellis in series 19.

'They remind me to work hard every single day.'

As the new series gets underway, Giovanni has his eye on the Grand Final once again – but is taking it one step at a time.

'This year, I just want to have a good time,' he says. 'I know Amanda's got potential and all I want to do is to make sure that she's going to be the best she can. I would love to see us going all the way and if it happens, it happens. If it doesn't, however far she gets, she's going to have a good time.'

Strictl

Ever wondered what a cucaracha looks like or how to spot a New Yorker? With our handy A to Z of *Strictly* you can become an instant expert – and start your own Saturday-night judging panel from the comfort of your living room.

A is for American Spin

A common move in the Jive, which originated from the Lindy Hop. The leader draws their hand across at waist height in the opposite direction to the spin, then flicks their hand back to the left and lets go to indicate to the follower that they should spin. While the follower is rotating, the leader can also choose to spin themselves, typically in an anticlockwise direction.

B is for Botafogo

Named after a coastal neighbourhood in Rio de Janeiro, Brazil, the botafogo is a Samba step, which starts on the diagonal and consists of a forward walk, swivelling through a quarter-turn, then putting the weight on the front, bent leg, then sidestepping with a quarter-swivel and then returning the weight to the first leg. During

C is for Cucaracha

The cucaracha is a classic Rumba step where each dancer steps to the side, then transfers their weight back to the original foot, then closes their feet, while moving the hips in a figure of eight. It literally translates as 'cockroach'.

D is for Double Reverse Spin

The double reverse spin is a full left (counter-clockwise) turn in one measure of music. It is danced in the Waltz, Quickstep and Tango.

onary

E is for Enchufla
A dance movement common in Salsa, where two partners begin by facing each other, then swap positions. Contact with one or two hands is maintained while the partners rotate 180 degrees around the same point.

F is for Fleckerl
A step found in the Viennese Waltz. Unlike the natural and reverse turns, the fleckerl does not move forwards along the dance floor but instead rotates on the spot. It can also be danced clockwise or counter-clockwise (natural or reverse), and the basic shape lasts for six steps.

G is for Gancho
One for fans of the Argentine Tango, a gancho is a sharp move when a dancer hooks a leg around their partner's leg by bending the knee and then straightening.

H is for Heel Lead
The Waltz, Tango, Foxtrot, Quickstep, Paso Doble and Viennese Waltz require a heel lead. When stepping forward, the dancer rolls from the back of the foot (the heel) towards the toe, without picking the foot up from the floor.

I is for Inside Turn
The individual turn of a partner in a Latin dance. There are many variations, but in its basic form a couple turn 180 degrees, but in the second turn the follower executes a 1.5 counter-clockwise (reverse) spin. A common move in Swing and Salsa.

J is for Jive Chassé
Pronounced 'Sha-say'. A triple-step to the side where one foot 'chases' the other in a 'step-together-step' pattern.

K is for Kick Ball Change
A two-step move where you step either back or to the side, transferring your weight onto the ball of that foot, then transfer your weight back onto your original foot. The kick ball change, as the name suggests, is when the dancer kicks before the ball change.

L is for Lock Step

The lock step, often seen in a Cha-cha-cha, Waltz, Quickstep, Foxtrot and Tango, refers to a series of movements where one foot is crossed behind the other and the front foot moves forward while the back foot stays 'locked' behind.

M is for Mambo

A Latin genre of dance first made popular in the clubs of Havana, Cuba, in the 1940s, and which emphasised free movement and feeling the music. Elements of the Mambo are found in modern-day Salsa.

N is for New Yorker

A common step found in the Cha-cha-cha and Rumba. The dancers break away from each other, turning 90 degrees to face the same way and sometimes extending the free arm, then come together and repeat in the opposite direction.

O is for Outside Turn

An individual 1.5 turn by one partner, exactly the same as an Inside Turn (see 'I is for Inside Turn'), but in a clockwise direction.

P is for Promenade Position

Seen in many ballroom dances, the promenade position is a V-shaped dance position in hold, with the leader's right hip touching the follower's left hip, with the other side slightly open. The direction of travel, and the position of the head, is towards the open side.

Q is for Quick, Slow

One of the basics of ballroom is learning to count out the steps in various combinations of these two speeds. In simple terms, slow means two beats and quick means one beat.

R is for Rondé

A toe of the straight leg draws a semicircle on the floor, and the foot or leg may be lifted off the floor. In ballroom dances the direction is usually from the front to back.

S is for Suzie Q

A Salsa step where the feet perform alternating cross steps and side steps with swivel action. The right foot crosses the left foot with the weight on the heel and the toe in the air. On beat two, the right toe swivels to the right while the left foot performs a small step to the side and the weight is transferred. The name originates from the US dance halls of the 1930s and was popularised in the 1936 song 'Doin' the Suzie Q' by Lil Hardin Armstrong.

T is for Toe Lead

While most ballroom dances require heel leads (see 'H is for Heel Lead'), Latin numbers require toe or ball leads, which improve floor connection and help the dancer change direction and add Latin hip action.

U is for Underarm Turn

A simple turn to the left or right, on the spot, performed by the following partner under a raised left hand–right hand hold. The turn is made to the left as the leading partner steps forward and to the right as they step back.

V is for Volta

Voltas come in three basic varieties. A travelling volta involves repeated side-cross movements (e.g. moving to the left with the right foot crossing and vice versa). In circular voltas the same side-cross movement is used to dance around an imaginary circle, and in a spot volta, a 360-degree turn on the spot is achieved with two cross-step motions.

W is for Weave

The natural weave (right-turning) and basic weave (left-turning) are commonly found in the Foxtrot, Quickstep and Waltz and consist of a pattern of six steps, danced mostly on the toes. In a basic weave, the lead steps forward with the left foot, then steps to the side with their right foot with an 1/8 of a turn. The lead then places their left foot behind the right foot, with an 1/8 turn, then takes the right foot back, then places the left to the side and slightly forward, and finally positions the left foot in front of the right outside their partner, taking a half-turn to the left.

X is for Xmas

The Christmas special is one of the highlights of the *Strictly* year and sees six celebrities battling it out on the dance floor, dancing to festive tunes. The perfect cherry on the *Strictly* cake.

Y is for Yolanda Tango

Frank Veloz and Yolanda Casazza were an American husband-and-wife dance team who were huge stars in the 1930s and 1940s. Their signature dance was the Yolanda Tango, which included a spectacular lift where Frank would pick up Yolanda, spin her with her head down, then throw her out as she landed on one knee in a low lunge, back leg extended.

Z is for Zumba

Not a term you'll ever hear on the show, but Zumba is a fitness programme inspired by Latin dance – it's a great way to get moving, and keeeeeeep dancing!

Going into her twenty-first series as host of *Strictly Come Dancing*, Tess is more excited than ever – it's even kept her awake at night.

'The launch show was such a buzz because we have a great collection of fizzy personalities in the class of '23,' she says. 'On the night of the show, I couldn't sleep because I kept waking up remembering things the celebrities had said and I'd find myself laughing out loud. Collectively, I genuinely feel these guys are going to be dynamite, and it's a real mixed bag of personalities. We have television royalty, soap stars, actors, presenters and sports personalities. Ellie Leach, who played Faye Windass in *Coronation Street* for half her life, told me her character had barely been able to crack a smile in the 12 years she was on the show and *Strictly* is the most fun she's ever had. That seemed to sum up the mood. The buzz was tangible. If their dancing is half as good as their chat, we are onto a winner.'

The sparkling new series follows hard on the heels of the spectacular series-20 Final and, while all four celebs were worthy of the Glitterball trophy, Tess says Hamza Yassin embodied the *Strictly* story.

'Hamza was my winner from week four when he did the Salsa, and he lifted Jowita, tossed her in the air and caught her,' she says. 'It was a moment I'll never forget. I'm not sure we'd ever seen that raw talent. As a wildlife filmmaker, he was used to holding cameras in his arms in the Arctic rather than a partner on the shiny dance floor, but he was a natural.

'He epitomises what *Strictly* is about. We soon got to know him and he is such an adorable personality, we took him into our hearts, but he also blew us away with his talent. It was a brilliant Final and all four were amazing.'

Apart from Hamza's Salsa, Tess's stand-out moment was Fleur East's Destiny's Child tribute, at Blackpool, which had the whole crew 'jumping'.

'The costume, the attitude she brought, it was so exciting,' she says. 'That was a real moment. And Dave Arch brought the medley to life. It's not easy, matching Destiny's Child, but Dave Arch can pull anything off and wows us every time.

'Fleur survived the dance-offs to reach the Final through sheer talent and hard work and now she's hosting *It Takes Two*. She's an inspired choice because she has walked in those footsteps and understands the mindset of the celebrities who have taken on this mammoth task. I think Fleur will be brilliant.'

With four incredible dancers in Hamza, Fleur, Helen Skelton and Molly Rainford, the Grand Final was closely contested and, for Tess, the showdance was key.

'It was a close-fought Final,' she says. 'We couldn't call it, because it's so much about the showdance and how the audience reacts. The showdance is a very personal tribute to your own dance journey and, personally, I want to be wowed, I want to be floored with your ability. I want to see everything you've learned and I want to see huge, exciting, jaw-dropping lifts. Often, it's the showdance that clinches the title of *Strictly* champion.'

With the new recruits, Tess is not offering any predictions just yet.

'It's anyone's game at this point, so I'm looking forward to seeing who blows our mind on the dance floor. I think it's going to be an exciting and unpredictable series.'

Tess Daly

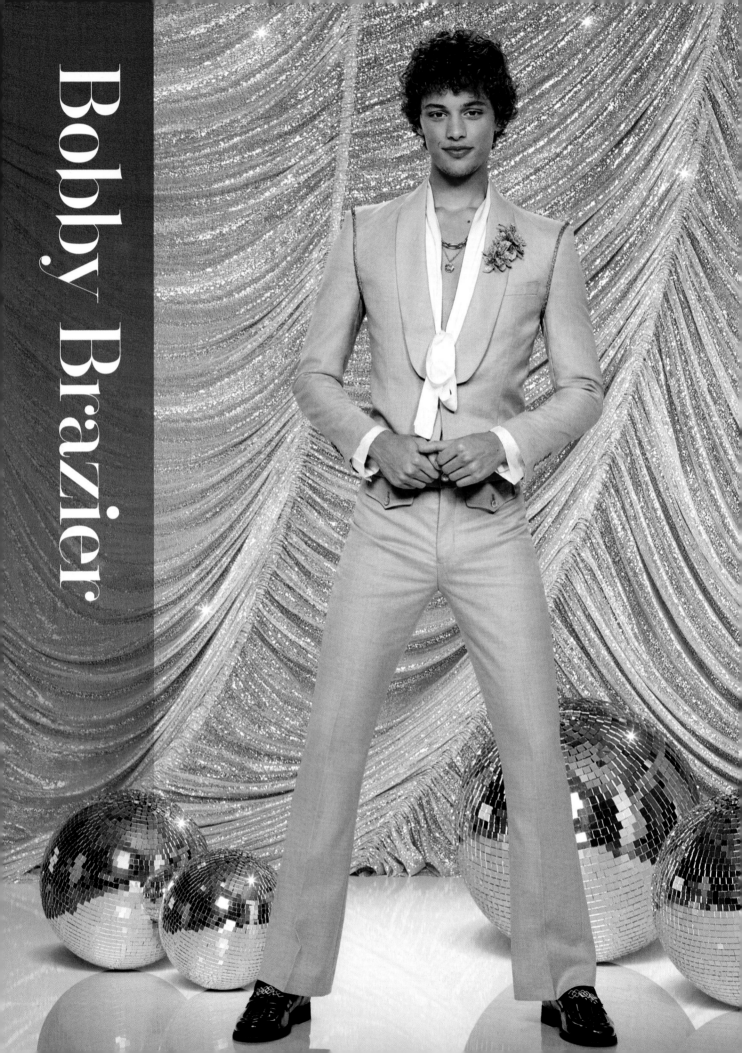

Bobby Brazier

He's the latest resident of Albert Square and has just landed his first National Television Award, now the *EastEnders* star promises to be a real bobby-dazzler on the dance floor.

'I'm really excited for the whole journey with my partner, Dianne Buswell, and everyone else involved,' he says. 'It's going to be sweet. There will be lots of ups and lots of downs, and I'm ready to feel all of it to the fullest extent. I love dancing, so the opportunity to dance with a professional and learn a different style every week is my idea of a good time.'

Partner Dianne might have her work cut out teaching Bobby the names of each dance, as well as the steps, but he's more than ready to put in the work.

'I don't know if I prefer Latin or ballroom,' he says. 'I like to move my hips and my shoulders, but I don't know the names of the dances. I know the Charleston, and that seems to be fun, with loads of energy, so I'm looking forward to that. But whatever I'm dancing, I want to make people feel what I'm feeling, whether it's fun or emotional. That is what's going to be great about *Strictly*, for me.'

Bobby, who appeared in reality shows alongside his late mum Jade Goody as a child, was scouted by a modelling agency at 16 and has walked the runway for fashion house Dolce & Gabbana at Milan Fashion Week, as well as having modelled for Tommy Hilfiger. In September, he took on the role of Freddie Slater in *EastEnders* and recently bagged the Rising Star award at the NTAs.

Dad Jeff and brother Freddie will be among those cheering Bobby on as he takes to the dance floor, and he says *Strictly* was always top of his TV wish list.

'My family are excited for me,' he says. 'Everybody who knows and loves me is really happy for me because they know that I'm going to really enjoy myself. I love to dance, so if there's any show that I'm going to do, it's *Strictly*.

'My *EastEnders* co-star James Bye, who did the show last year, told me to be myself – and eat a lot!'

Used to modelling the latest fashions on the catwalks of Paris and London, Bobby is happy to take on as much glam and glitter as the costume department can throw at him.

'I'm ready to take it all in my stride,' he says. 'It's all part of doing *Strictly*. I think it will make it even more fun. Dancing to music that I enjoy is going to be great, but doing it in a costume that fits the energy of the song and the dance is even better. It's just one big performance and I'm a performer.'

Although Bobby's favourite week is Halloween – and he jokes his perfect look would be a 'handsome devil' – there's another show in the series he's set as his benchmark.

'I'm aiming for the Grand Final,' he laughs. 'I always like to try my best!'

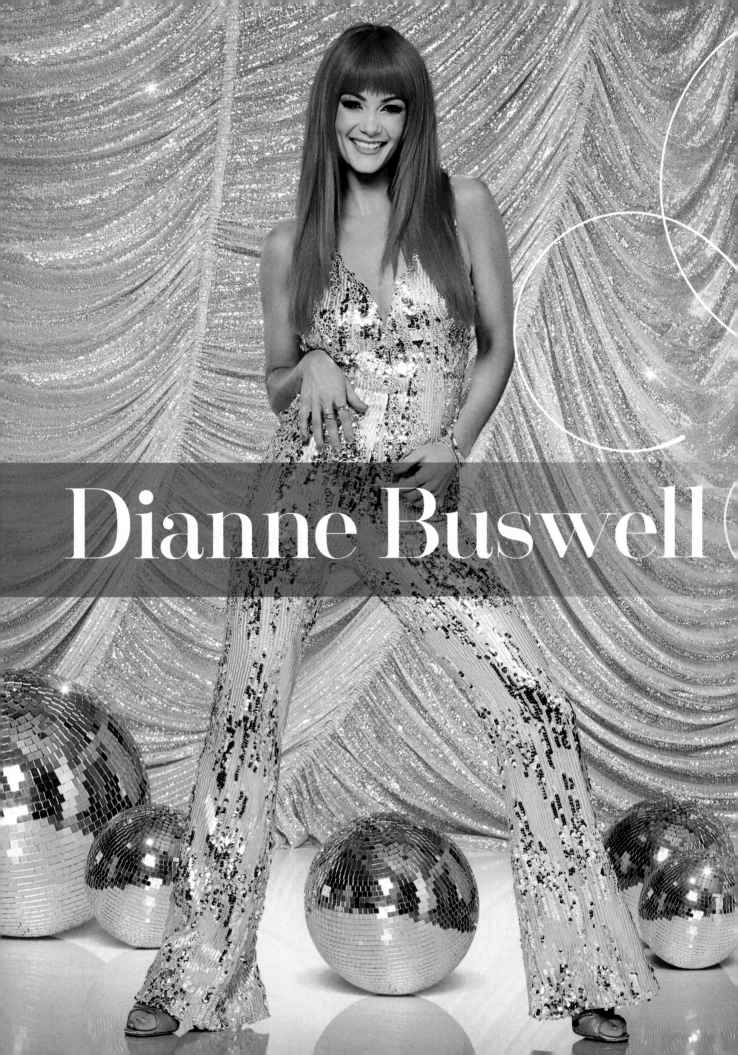

Dianne Buswell

Former finalist Dianne put *EastEnders* star Bobby Brazier through his paces when they met on the Albert Square set and says what he lacks in knowledge he makes up for in personality and natural talent.

'Bobby is that person that you watch dance and you can't help but smile, even if he's doing it wrong! It's early days and Bobby has never even heard of the ballroom dances, let alone danced them, but he's got so much natural talent. He has never done anything like this, but had he started dancing at a young age, he could have been one of the best. He's a natural mover but everything is new. We're having a lot of fun and he's such a sweet boy.'

The pair kicked off their series with a Foxtrot and, although Bobby has said he is more suited to the freer Latin style, Dianne thinks ballroom could be his forte.

'Bobby thought he would be best at the Latin styles, but I beg to differ,' she says. 'He's proving himself to be quite the ballroom boy. Don't get me wrong, I think he's going to be great at the Latin, but I think deep down he loves the whole sophistication of the ballroom.

'When we started he didn't know the difference between Latin and ballroom, or any of the dance names. But I told him it's my job to teach him all about it. I'm excited to teach him and watch him grow as a dancer.'

The former Australian Open Champion and four-time Amateur Australian Open finalist danced with brother Andrew from a young age. She competed as a pro dancer on the Australian version of *Strictly Come Dancing* in 2015 and two years later moved over to the UK series, dancing with the Reverend Richard Coles. In series 16, she reached the Final with social media star Joe Sugg and last year she made up team TyDi with DJ Tyler West, dancing through to Blackpool week.

'Tyler was great. He had a lot of natural dance ability,' she says. 'He was a complete novice but he had music as his background so he understood the timing and the intricacies of the music, which helped a lot. He was a great student and worked super hard.

'Looking back, I think we could have gone a bit further, but at the same time, the competition last year was so strong that if it wasn't us, it would have been another good competitor. We felt we left on a really good dance, our Salsa, so we went out on a high.'

The Australian dancer says she and Tyler became firm friends over their *Strictly* journey.

'TyDi was amazing, we had such a good time,' she says. 'It's really special when you get someone you connect with, because you're spending so much time teaching them and they can become friends for life. I feel really grateful for that.'

Hoping to take Bobby through to the Grand Final, Dianne says her new partner is an enthusiastic pupil.

'It will be fun working with Bobby and watching him improve as a dancer,' she says. 'I want him to learn as many dances as he can get under his belt, because he loves dancing so much. When someone loves what they're doing as much as I do, it gives me so much joy. My favourite thing is going to be watching him enjoy the moment.'

Krishnan Guru-Murthy

One of the nation's most trusted TV journalists, Krishnan is swapping hard news for dancing shoes and says he is finding the switch 'exhilarating'.

'I finally realised that the chance to do *Strictly* was an opportunity to inject some joy into my very serious career,' he says. 'The news has been especially serious in the last few years and, as a news presenter, you feel at the centre of it, so it's quite high pressure. The opportunity to have an outlet, which is so all-consuming, is too good to miss. You can't think about anything else when you're dancing. You shouldn't even think about dancing when you're dancing – you should just dance. So it's like a holiday from everything else. Even when I'm dancing in the morning and delivering the news in the evening, I feel more refreshed afterwards.'

Born in Liverpool, Krishnan started his TV career presenting youth programmes on the BBC before fronting *Newsround* for three years, from 1991. He moved on to *Newsnight* and, in 1997, he was one of the launch presenters for BBC News 24. A year later, he joined the Channel 4 team, where he is now the main news anchor, and has covered major events. He also commentates on live events for Channel 4, such as the Paralympics ceremonies, hosts live election debates and presents documentaries. Krishnan won the Royal Television Society Television Journalism Award for Network Presenter of the Year in 2022.

The dad-of-two, who is partnered with professional dancer Lauren Oakley, says his family are thrilled he's taken on the *Strictly* challenge and can't wait to watch.

'My mum is delighted,' he says. 'She's really enthusiastic about me doing *Strictly* and thinks it's fantastic. Everyone's really positive about it in my family except my 16-year-old son, who is as embarrassed about it as you'd expect a 16-year-old boy to be!'

The news hound says his biggest challenge at the moment is 'learning to do more than one thing at a time', but he is determined to give it his all. And after decades of interviewing everyone from prime ministers to pop stars, Krishnan is relishing the chance to leave his notebook at home while he gets to know his fellow contestants.

'It's great hanging out with this bunch of people,' he says. 'I might meet Annabel Croft at Wimbledon, I've met Les Dennis and I've interviewed Jody Cundy once, but there's no way I would normally get to spend time and have fun with this amazing crowd.'

A familiar face to millions through the Channel 4 news, Krishnan is keen to reveal the less serious side of his nature.

'I like to think that, because I've been around so long, people have grown up with me and know that I'm a rounded human being and capable of enjoying life. Since the advent of social media, I've given away a lot of who I am and what I do out of work, but *Strictly* is more extreme. I hope viewers will be on the journey with me as I discover that side of myself.'

With a work wardrobe full of sober suits, Krishnan is also ready to sparkle.

'I'm embracing the glitz full-on,' he says. 'I was initially very boring about it, saying, "There'll be no glitter and sequins," but now I'm very much "Bring it on. There aren't enough sequins on that!"'

Lauren Oakley

After joining the *Strictly* professionals team last year, Lauren is dancing with her first celebrity partner in series 21, and the good news is that it's Krishnan Guru-Murthy.

'I'm so excited. I can't wait to get into the studio and throw myself into this year,' she says. 'I'm looking forward to having the full *Strictly* experience.'

While Krishnan is usually seen sitting behind a desk, looking serious, Lauren believes viewers are about to see a whole new side of the Channel 4 newsreader.

'Krishnan has really groovy moves and he's definitely got rhythm, so it's just about adding the choreography and getting his natural rhythm into the steps,' she says. 'He may be more of a ballroom natural, but I think the audience will be quite surprised with his Latin as well. He's definitely got the hips.

'As a newsreader Krishnan works in a serious environment, but he really wants to dive in and give it a go. He's a really hard worker and I think he's ready to let his inner dancer burst out.'

Lauren hopes Krishnan's long and distinguished career in journalism will stand him in good stead for the live shows.

'He is used to staying calm under pressure because news shows are live, which will help. Plus, he's been around television studios for 30 years, so he's used to the environment. In fact, he started *Newsround* the year I was born, which we thought was hilarious. Also, the audience don't often get to see his joyful side, and dance is a way to have a laugh, rush headlong into something and just be yourself. All of those qualities will help him in the competition.'

Born in Birmingham, into a ballroom family, Lauren was dancing at two and competing at seven, winning her first World Championship at the age of nine. She is two-time UK Under 21 Latin champion, British Under 21 Latin champion and UK and British Under 21 Ballroom champion. Now in her second *Strictly* series, Lauren says she is grateful to have had a year to learn the ropes before taking on a celebrity partner.

'When you watch it at home, you see the finished product, but being there in the studio, you see the whole machine that is *Strictly*,' she says. 'My first year was a lovely, gentle introduction, being involved in all the group dances and the music acts and seeing how amazing all the other pros were with their celebs. It was a great way to show me what I need to do now it is my turn.'

Lauren knew most of the pros before joining the show, and says she was welcomed with open arms.

'Normally the first day in a new job, you don't know what to expect, but I was really lucky because I already knew the people I was working with and we all just picked up where we left off, which was lovely.

'I really enjoyed being part of the group dances and I loved Blackpool and Musicals Week, because I was part of so many dance numbers, so it was like dance, quick change, dance, quick change. It was really exciting. I loved getting to know the celebs and supporting them every week.

'My first year was a dream come true because I've grown up watching the show. Every corner I turned I was thinking, "Oh my gosh, I'm here. Pinch me!"'

Now in the training room with her celebrity partner, Lauren says she will not be cracking the whip too hard.

'As a teacher I'm quite calm and patient,' she says. 'I think the foundation of dance is to enjoy it and your body responds and moves better when you're having fun, like when you're on a night out,' she says. 'The celebrities are out of their comfort zone, dancing in front of millions of people, so the most important thing is for them to feel comfortable and confident, and then I will get the best out of them. So I'm patient and kind, but with a deadline, if I have to get strict, I will!'

1 What surname was shared by three contestants in series 20 and one in series 18? And can you name them all? *(5 points)*

3 Who is the longest-serving current *Strictly* pro? *(1 point)*

2 Rose Ayling-Ellis stole the nation's heart with her Couple's Choice in 2021, but can you name the track she danced to? *(1 point)*

Strictly

Test your *Strictly* knowledge with our all-singing, all-dancing quiz. A total of 23 points is available, and if you get over 20, you're officially a *Strictly* Superfan.

4 Now one of the show's esteemed judges, Anton Du Beke danced with celebrity contestants for 18 series. But who was his last *Strictly* partner? *(1 point)*

5 Which special anniversary was marked in 2022 with a themed week in series 20? *(1 point)*

6 Which *Strictly* judge dressed as Morticia Addams for the 2022 Halloween Week? *(1 point)*

7 Which three of the show's professionals hail from Italy? *(1 point each)*

8 Who scored a perfect 40 for her Destiny's Child-inspired Couple's Choice at Blackpool in series 20, and repeated the feat in the Grand Final? *(1 point)*

9 Which American singing legend became a guest judge in 2014? *(1 point)*

10 Which ballroom-based *Strictly* dance style allows lifts? *(1 point)*

Quiz

11 Which celebrity danced a Cha-cha-cha to the theme from *Fame* in 2022's Musicals Week? *(1 point)*

12 Three sports personalities have walked away with the Glitterball trophy since 2004. Can you name them all? *(1 point each)*

13 Which *Coronation Street* actor won the 2022 Christmas special with her Quickstep to 'Sleigh Ride'? *(1 point)*

14 Who famously danced to 'Gangnam Style' in 2016? *(1 point)*

15 Which celebrity champion was joined on the dance floor by an augmented reality elephant for his Dr Doolittle themed Quickstep? *(1 point)*

Eddie Kadi

As a comedian and presenter, Eddie has had many career highs, including being the first Black British comedian to headline London's O2 Arena. And he says being asked to do *Strictly Come Dancing* is another huge goal to tick off the list.

'I'm so excited, I feel like a child,' he says. 'My family all love *Strictly*, so for me this is a dream. I love dancing. I've never done it professionally, but I'm first on the dance floor at weddings and birthday parties, and I danced in assembly in primary school. I'm looking forward to learning new moves, especially the Latin dances, like the Salsa. I can't wait.'

Born in Kinshasa, Democratic Republic of the Congo, Eddie moved to West London with his family when he was eight. He fell into performing by chance, after being asked to host a talent showcase at university, and in 2006 he was named Best Newcomer at the Black Entertainment Comedy Awards. Since then, he has been packing out comedy venues and starring in numerous TV shows, including, *Sorry, I Didn't Know*, *QI* and *Richard Osman's House of Games*. He has also hosted the prestigious MOBO Awards and produced a Channel 4 documentary on Africa. He is a prolific podcaster as well as presenting Radio 1's *Afrobeats Chart Show*. Now he wants to bring some of his African roots to the *Strictly* dance floor.

'That is part of me, so if I get any opportunity, I'm bringing the African vibes,' he says. 'My dad is waiting for those moves, so if I don't, I'll be in trouble!'

'My dad has been with me from the start of that journey to becoming a comedian, and I had to convince him that this is a good career, but every time a new thing happens in my life, he's just so proud. When I was offered the show, he said he had been waiting for me to do *Strictly*. He is my biggest fan, so it's a very emotional stage for me and my dad.'

The multitalented star – who is paired with Karen Hauer – is looking forward to adding a new string to his bow and says he will welcome the critique from the judges.

'Feedback is my best friend,' he says. 'In terms of my stand-up, having my colleagues around was great and I'm a really good listener. I don't see it as criticism, just a way of helping us do better.

'In terms of the *Strictly* professional dancers, we have the best dancers in the world teaching us how to dance. That's such a beautiful thing, so I will be listening to Karen and trying my best.'

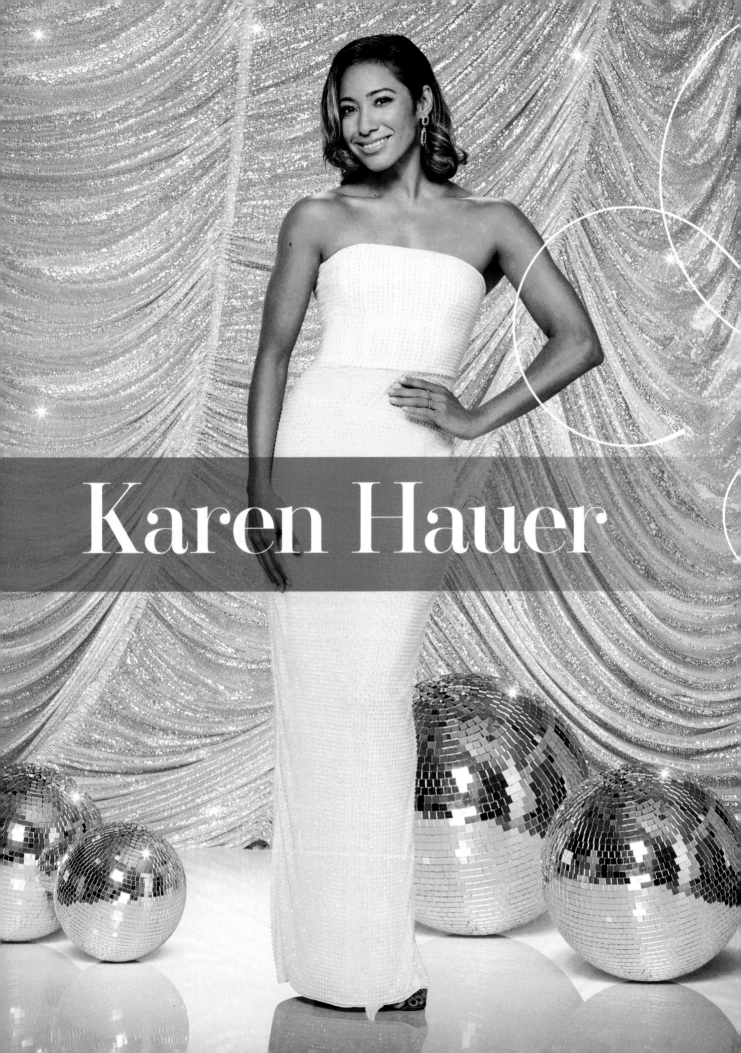

Karen Hauer

Strictly's longest-serving current professional dancer Karen is on top of the world after meeting comedian Eddie Kadi on the roof of the O2 Arena to reveal their partnership, and she is hoping to take him to new heights in the competition.

'When we did the reveal we were both screaming,' she says. 'We meet the celebrities in group rehearsals beforehand and Eddie and I got along very well – he was very easy to speak to. He has natural energy. What I've always loved about the start of the series, when you get a new celebrity, is their energy and their enthusiasm, and he's got bundles of that.'

Her new partner is already showing some aptitude on the dance floor, although he's never had any formal training.

'Eddie's got musicality, and my job is to hone that,' she says. 'In rehearsals, he told me he now has a lot more respect for dancing. He can throw a couple of shapes in a club, but when you start learning the technique, it's a completely different ballgame.'

With Eddie originally hailing from the Democratic Republic of the Congo, he is keen to bring his African roots to the *Strictly* floor and Karen is happy to tap into that.

'When we do the Latin dances, I can incorporate the way he feels music, which is lovely,' she says.

'We started with a Quickstep, which is one of the hardest ballroom dances to start with. Everyone struggles with the frame, the bounce and the changes in rhythm, but I had time, in the first two weeks, to hone those little details that will help throughout the series.'

The Venezuelan-born dancer first found her passion for dancing at eight, after moving to New York, winning a scholarship to the Martha Graham School of Contemporary Dance. She studied African dance, contemporary dance and ballet before specialising in ballroom and Latin at 19. In 2008, she was crowned World Mambo Champion and a year later Rising Star Professional American Rhythm Champion. Since joining *Strictly* in 2012, she has reached the Final twice, with Mark Wright and Jamie Laing. Last year, she partnered comedian Jayde Adams.

'Dancing with Jayde was a new experience,' she says. 'It challenged me to think outside the box with the choreography and we created some great numbers, including the *Flashdance* routine. A lot of people loved that because it gave a great message about body positivity. We got lovely messages from the public.'

As a *Strictly* stalwart of 11 years, Karen has cast a seasoned eye over the new recruits and is looking forward to seeing who makes the grade over the coming weeks.

'It's an outstanding line-up with great characters and some lovely dancers,' she says. 'I can't wait to see who throws themselves into the challenge.'

Having seen many a finalist lift the Glitterball trophy, Karen has a fair idea what makes a champion.

As she embarks on her latest *Strictly* series, Karen says she wants to give Eddie an experience he'll never forget.

'My previous celebrity partners have said *Strictly* has been the most eye-opening journey of self-discovery,' she says. 'It goes beyond teaching them to dance. You learn determination, build confidence and learn things about yourself. I want all the people I dance with to see that they can do anything they put their minds to.'

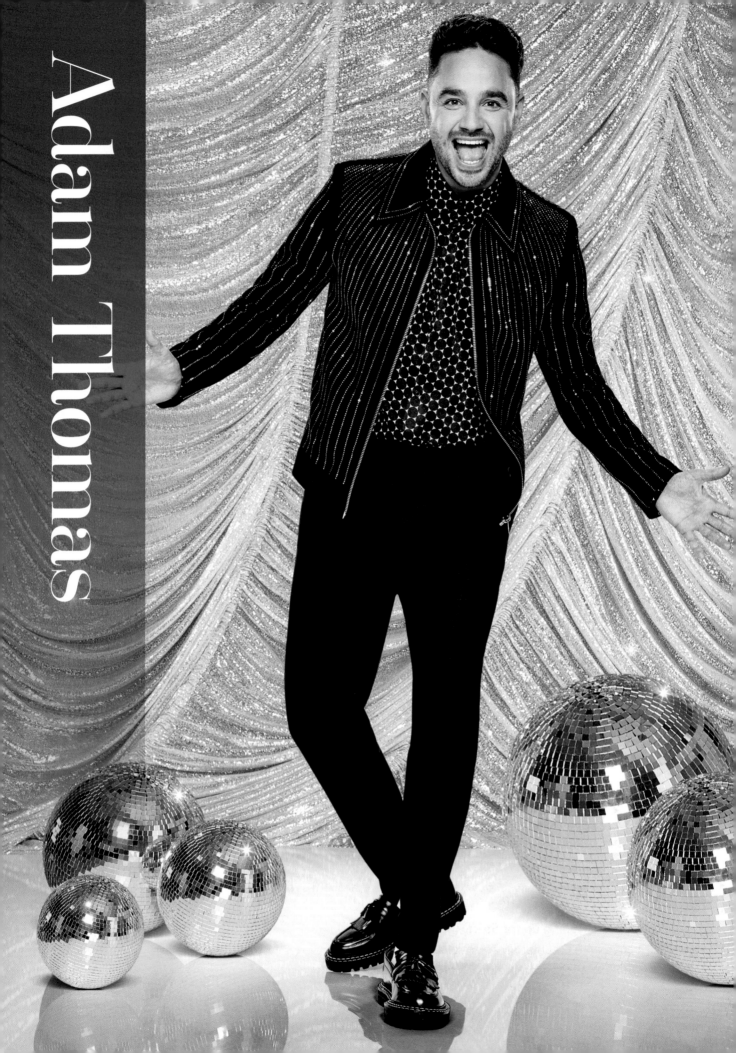

Adam Thomas

Waterloo Road star Adam Thomas is thrilled to be joining the class of 2023 and says he's been an avid viewer of *Strictly* for years, along with the rest of his family. As he swaps the fictional school for lessons from new tutor Luba Mushtuk, he reveals some special cheerleaders will be watching every weekend.

'My wife, Caroline, and the kids are huge fans of the show,' he says. 'My little boy, Teddy, is nine and my little girl, Elsie, is five, and they couldn't be more excited. They'll be cheering me on. I can't dance to save my life but I'm buzzing to learn.

'The fact that my wife is a dance teacher and I have never learnt how to dance just baffles me, but she said that I haven't taught her how to act either. I have had no dance experience so this is definitely a first for me, but again, I am excited to learn and have a good laugh with Luba. Get me on that dance floor!'

Mancunian Adam landed his breakthrough role in the original series of school drama *Waterloo Road* at the age of 18, playing bad boy Donte Charles for three years, until 2009. He went on to play Adam Barton in ITV soap *Emmerdale*, winning a *TV Choice* award for Best Soap Newcomer. He headed into the jungle for *I'm a Celebrity … Get Me Out of Here!* in 2016 before co-hosting the spin-off series, *I'm a Celebrity: Extra Camp*. In 2021, he returned to the role of Donte on the rebooted *Waterloo Road*.

Adam often works with his brothers, former *Coronation Street* star Ryan and *Love Island* star Scott, and in 2020 they made the ITV travel series *Absolutely India: Mancs in Mumbai*, when they took their late father back to India to trace their heritage.

Shortly before signing up for *Strictly*, Adam was diagnosed with rheumatoid arthritis, and he says this is one of the reasons he has taken on the challenge.

'The diagnosis is a blessing because I was in a lot of pain and I didn't know what was up with me,' he says. 'Now I finally do, I can put an action in place to get it under control. It's been a bit of a tough year for the family, but they're happy I'm doing *Strictly* and it's the right time for me.

'I wanted to do the show because of my own little personal journey and I want my family to enjoy it. I also want to get out there on that dance floor and move because I feel like I've not for a long time.'

The actor has recently been seeking advice from *Waterloo Road* co-star Kym Marsh and says he now understands how hard she was working when she appeared on *Strictly* last year.

'Kym was doing the show, coming to work to film scenes, then going back to training, but if you're not in the bubble, you don't realise what's going on,' he says. 'Now I understand what a commitment that was. Everyone has told me it's hard work, but hard work never hurt anyone. Kym and everyone who's been on the show that I've spoken to says they had the best time ever and that it's going to be great, so just enjoy every second.'

After eyeing up the competition, the TV star says he's impressed with his fellow celebrities.

'I am going to be honest, when I first joined the show, I thought I had a shot at it,' he says. 'But now I have seen the competition and I know what I am up against!

'That has actually made me feel a lot more at ease, because I am not necessarily in it to win it now. I am just here to enjoy it and have fun. If it happens it happens, but it really shouldn't happen. I am just going to take every dance as it comes and see how we get on.'

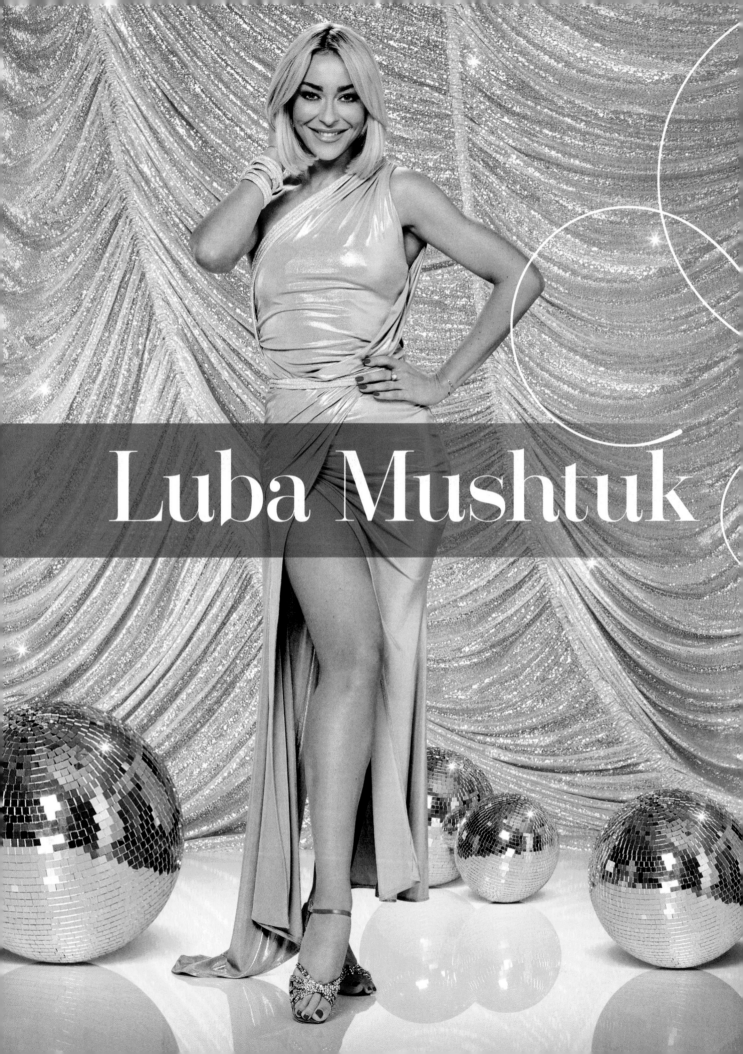

Luba Mushtuk

Paired with actor Adam Thomas for the forthcoming series, Luba is over the moon and says she's expecting to have a lot of fun.

'I'm the happiest person on the planet at the moment and hopefully will stay that way for many, many weeks,' she laughs. 'Adam is such a bubbly, joyful person to be around, so I'm super-pleased and honoured to be paired with him. He really enjoyed the launch show and, after going through the mini-choreography we had for the group dance, I think he's going to be just fine. His strength will be his infectious smile and the joy that he brings onto the dance floor.'

As a teacher, Luba is looking forward to putting the *Waterloo Road* star through his paces in the classroom – and she promises to be firm but fair.

'I think every person needs something different and I need to take time to see what works best with Adam,' she says. 'He's an actor, not a sportsman, so my approach will be very different to previous celebrity partners, who came from the world of sport. You do need to put in the hours and you need repetition for the muscle memory to function, so there is an aspect of discipline. At the same time, I truly want him to have the best time and enjoy it.'

Since last year, Luba has been taking acting lessons in her spare time, and she is hoping to hone those skills with her thespian partner.

'Being an actor, he can create incredible characters, so I want to create sort of a mini-film in each choreography,' she says. 'I adore Movie Week and I've fallen in love with acting, so maybe this year I will get the opportunity to show off what I've been learning. Perhaps Adam can teach me as well.'

Russian-born Luba moved to Italy at 12 to study dance under legendary teacher Caterina Arzenton and is four-time winner of the Italian Dance Championship and Italian Open Latin Show Dance champion. She joined the *Strictly* pro team in series 16 and has since partnered James Cracknell and Jason Bell. This year, she thinks viewers are in for a few surprises.

'The line-up is really strong,' she says. 'They look fantastic already and, with a professional eye, I can see there are quite a few dark horses, who you may not expect but who will be phenomenal. They're all lovely people. It's strange because everyone bonds so well – you don't feel that there's a competition at all. I always say I wish we just could go through the whole series without eliminating anyone, just like in week one.'

To be close to Adam's home and family, Luba will be training in Manchester, which she says is a 'beautiful city', and she's hoping the former *Emmerdale* star will be her ticket to the Grand Final.

'I really hope we get to the Final, but at the same time, it's about the process,' she says. 'It's about enjoying every single day and I do believe, in life as in *Strictly*, planning is pointless because life has made plans already. So I just want to enjoy every day, every rehearsal, every routine. It's a privilege to dance with him so I've already won!

'Adam's a joyful man who is very ambitious, and who really wants to make himself proud, his family proud and his kids proud. I'm here for all of that, each step of the way, guiding him. I think it will be a beautiful journey.'

Music, Maestro, Please

Without music, there would be no *Strictly*, and it remains the only prime-time show with its own live band.

Along with the four incredible singers, the 5-strong group of talented musicians, led by Musical Director Dave Arch, can turn their hand to any genre, from a rocking Queen number to a big-band standard or a slow, classical Waltz.

Before the first note is played on stage, Dave and Music Producer Ian Masterson work together to recreate each track in the 90-second format required for the couples' routines. While Ian works up a version that the pro and celeb dancers use in the rehearsal room, Dave writes the arrangement for the live band to play on Saturday night.

'Once we know what tracks are in the show, I take them away and reconstruct them to make them fit the tempo and style,' says Ian. 'So we turn a pop song into a Samba or Salsa or whatever is needed, because modern hits aren't always a perfect fit for the dance and require re-mixing to give the dancers something to

Work on the arrangements begins on Sunday, when the first of the tracks for the next live show are locked in. With each number, Dave strips back the layers and writes the musical script for the musicians and vocalists. 'Ian creates edits and adds accents for drums, etc., and I take the track and make it work for the live band,' he says. 'We have always adapted the music to fit the style, but the show has got more adventurous and there are now more tracks that are not genuine Tangos, for example.

'Writing the arrangement takes an average of four to five hours per track. If you have a slow solo piano tune, it won't take as long as an intricate, fast tune with a million notes.

'The choice of music is a collaboration between Ian, the pros, Creative Director Jason Gilkison, Executive Producer Sarah James and Series Editor Jack Gledhill. Tracks are suggested at a weekly production meeting and are planned to offer maximum variety on each show, but celebs also get a say.' The whole show is hugely collaborative,' says Ian. 'We work closely with the pro dancers, and a lot of the time they'll come to us with suggestions either from them we ask the celebrities about their favourite songs and anything that means a lot to them. For example, in the last series Will Mellor wanted to Waltz to "Three Times a Lady" in honour of his late dad, so we accommodated that. We don't just throw songs at people and tell them what to dance to. As we plan ahead, we have a mix in our heads of how the shows can evolve for each couple, and that starts with the dance styles. So if a couple starts with a Waltz – a ballroom dance – then they do Latin the next week, which could be a Samba or a Salsa. It's like a chessboard and we move the pieces to get the best possible performance for every couple. In any one week, I've got three shows in my head – the current week, the following week and the week after. At the beginning of the series, we have 15 couples and we don't know who will be eliminated, so I'm thinking about 45 tracks at once. It's quite busy!'

The *Strictly* band consists of eight brass instruments and a rhythm section – made up of two keyboards, two guitars, bass, drums and percussion. Incredibly, the first time they come together is on the Friday night before the show.

'The band and singers get together in the studio for three hours after the dance rehearsals, and that's the first time I hear what I've put down on paper,' says Dave. 'The singers are sent their parts so they can practise, and if there's anything really difficult, like flamenco guitar, I may send that to the musician in advance. But on the whole the band just turn

The couples only get to rehearse with the live band in the precious hours before the show, during Saturday rehearsals.'The couples get two run-throughs in the morning, then a dress rehearsal and the show.'

Between rehearsals, Dave joins Ian and the technical wizards in the sound gallery to make sure the levels are all working for the show. 'We record the rehearsals and take a snapshot of the mix for each track,' explains Dave. 'Then I go in to the sound gallery and listen back, to make sure the balance works for each song, because sonically they are all different.'

Ian says the reward for their hard work is in watching the beautiful routines unfold on the dance floor. 'It's lovely to be able to play a part in creating a performance,' he says. 'When you see something like Rose Ayling-Ellis and Giovanni Pernice's silent dance, it's an epic moment and the culmination of a massive team effort. I'm very proud of that, because it's not down to any one person – it's what we do on the show together that makes it happen.'

Les Dennis

One of the nation's best-loved entertainers, Les has been in showbusiness for over 50 years. Now he is marking a milestone birthday and says *Strictly* is the perfect way to celebrate.

'I got asked to come on the show and I thought, "Why not?" It's my seventieth birthday on 12 October and I love a challenge,' he says. 'I've recently done my first opera, with the English National Opera, and performed with the Royal Shakespeare Company, so I thought *Strictly* would be an excellent achievement to add to that – something outside of my comfort zone.'

The Liverpudlian comedian and presenter sprang to fame after winning talent show *New Faces* in 1974 and becoming a regular on *Russ Abbot's Madhouse* (later *The Russ Abbot Show*). He formed a double act with the late impressionist Dustin Gee, starring in *The Laughter Show*, before becoming the face of ITV's *Family Fortunes* for 15 years, from 1987. He has also had an illustrious acting career, starring in *Coronation Street* for two years and numerous theatre shows including *Chicago*, *Me and My Girl* and *Hairspray*. He recently starred as Sir Joseph in the English National Opera's production of *H.M.S. Pinafore* at the London Coliseum – and he says he is looking forward to dressing up in his finery for the *Strictly* dance floor.

'In *H.M.S. Pinafore* I had the full regalia, so I'm not afraid of the loud costumes,' he laughs. 'But the *Strictly* wardrobe department is great and they make sure every costume is right for you, so I'm happy to be in their expert hands.'

Although he has appeared in stage musicals, Les has no formal dance training. But he has been throwing himself into preparation for the show by upping his exercise regime.

'I consciously decided to put my fitness watch back on and get my 10,000 steps a day,' says Les. 'I've been working hard, not dancing, but trying to get myself fit. I really want to get to Movie Week, because I love movies. I love *The Godfather*. Maybe I could channel Marlon Brando and the dance he did with his daughter at the beginning of the film.'

In the meantime Les, paired with Nancy Xu, is itching to get started and enjoying the buzz of meeting the professional dancers and celebrities in the show. When it comes to his performance on the dance floor, he promises to give it his all.

'At the beginning I was nervous and excited, but now we're here, it's pure excitement and I am loving being a part of the *Strictly* family already.

'There's a lot to think about, like getting the steps right and the expression, making sure you look like you're having fun, not looking tense. But it's live telly. You've got to go for it. You have to give it 100 per cent.'

Dad-of-three Les says his family are all 'thrilled' he's become a *Strictly* star and, while he's already a household name, he's hoping to appeal to a whole new generation of fans. 'When people come up to me, it's usually the mum and dad who ask for selfies and the kids are looking at me like, "Who is that?"' he laughs. 'But now it will be, "We know who it is. He's the guy from *Strictly*."'

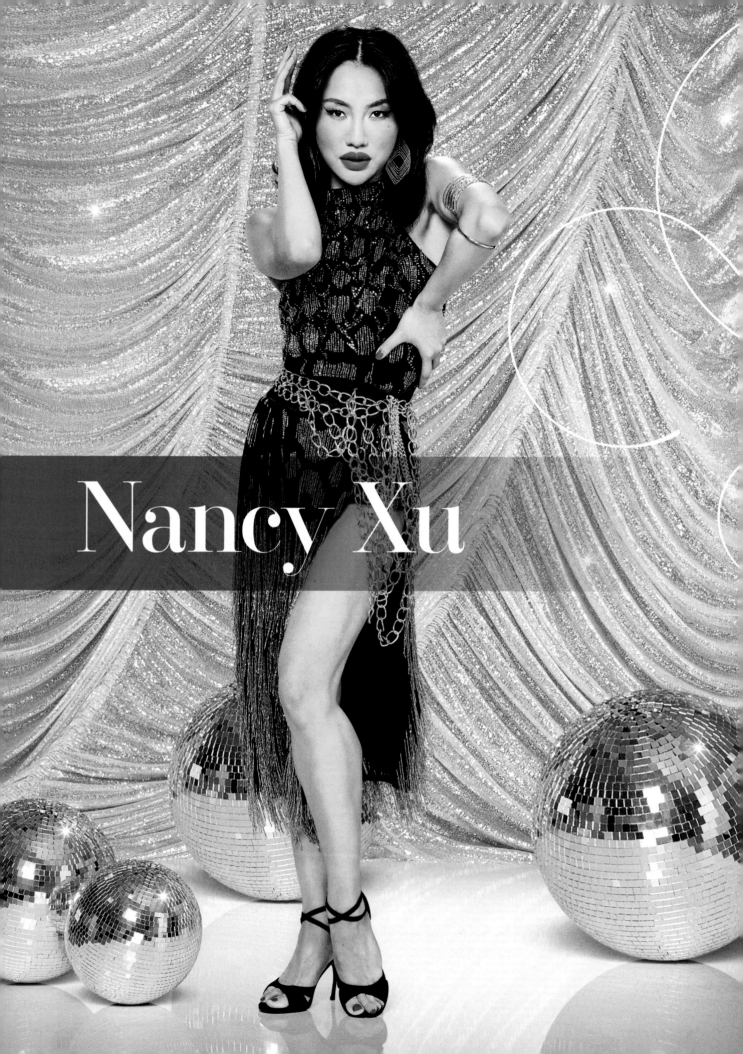

Nancy Xu

Nancy has previously hit the dance floor with presenter Rhys Stephenson and actor Will Mellor, making it to the Semi-finals both times. Now she is hoping it's third time lucky with comedian and actor Les Dennis.

'I'm very excited for everything to start,' she says. 'We are we training very hard. We'd love to get to the Final, but this show is about the journey and making sure the celebrity is enjoying themselves along the way.'

The pair kicked off the series with a Tango, and Nancy says Les shows promise in the ballroom dances, but it's not always easy for a novice to achieve the posture and technique required in the first few weeks.

'The audience may think we make it look easy on camera, but that's because we are actually working very hard,' she says. 'Each Latin and ballroom dance has specific details, and particular techniques, and those don't come naturally to everyone. With the Tango, for example, it's a ballroom dance and it's about the frame and the footwork. You have to remember to position the toe and lead with the heel and that's a lot of things for someone who has never danced ballroom and Latin before.

'I think the hardest thing for male celebrities and female professionals is that the man has to lead. As the pro, you have to always follow the leader, so I can't be pulling and pushing him in the dance.'

Nancy, who first met Les in his native Liverpool for the show, says the pair are getting on like a house on fire.

Born in China's Hunan province, Nancy began dancing at eight and has competed all over the world. She was runner-up at the 2013 International Singapore Championships, third place in the 2010–2012 CBDF National Amateur Latin Championships and a finalist in the U21 World Championships in 2010. She appeared in the Chinese version of *So You Think You Can Dance?* as well as *Burn the Floor* in both the West End and Broadway before joining *Strictly* in 2019. Her partnership with Will Mellor, last year, saw them top the leaderboard with their elegant Foxtrot in the Quarter-final before leaving the competition the following week.

'Will is a lovely man and we get on so well with each other,' she says. 'Like Rhys from the year before, we're still in touch. Before this series Will sent me a message saying, "Whoever you dance with this series, send them my best wishes. I'm going to be supporting you."'

As she begins her *Strictly* series with national treasure Les, Nancy is keen to make sure he has a ball.

'I would say this to all the celebs on *Strictly*: make sure you are enjoying the journey,' she says. 'It's a once-in-a-lifetime experience and it's going to be tough sometimes, especially if you want to get to do it correctly and you want to keep going with this journey. But if you cannot enjoy the present, you cannot enjoy the future. Enjoy the moment and have fun, that's the key.'

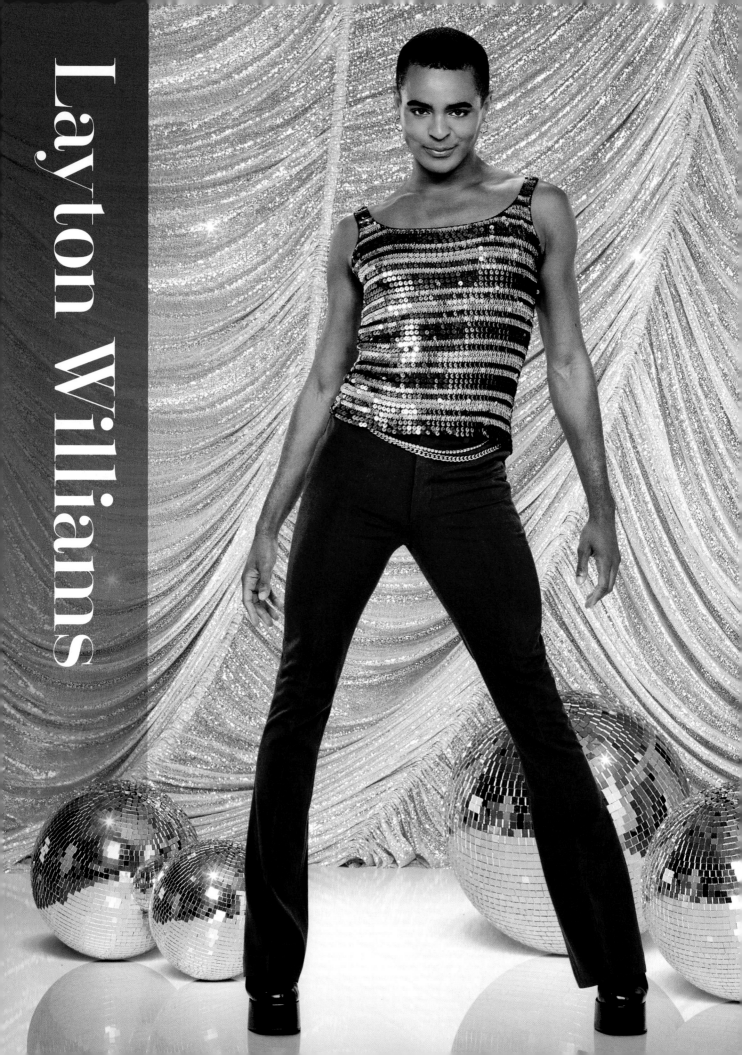

Layton Williams

Star of stage and screen Layton has been acting since he was a child, first taking the lead in *Billy Elliot the Musical* when he was just 12 years old. Now he is thrilled to be taking to the *Strictly* dance floor to learn a new skill.

'When *Strictly* comes around every year it's a big moment for me,' he says. 'So when I was asked to do the show I thought, "If I don't do it now, when am I going to do it?" I jumped at the chance to get dressed up and hit the dance floor. On the first day dancing with my partner I thought, "Oh my God, this is real now," but I loved it.'

Manchester-born Layton is best known to TV viewers as Stephen Carmichael in *Bad Education* and as 13-year-old dreamer Kylie in the 2009 series *Beautiful People*. His impressive stage career also saw him cast as a young Michael Jackson in *Thriller Live*, before starring in Matthew Bourne's *The Car Man* at Sadler's Wells and the twentieth-anniversary revival of *Rent*. Most recently he has taken the lead in the hit musical *Everybody's Talking About Jamie*. Despite his musical-theatre background, Layton says he has a lot to learn from *Strictly* partner Nikita Kuzmin.

'*Strictly* is a whole different world,' he says. 'You think it's going to be easy to do the Latin and ballroom steps, but they are different postures and a completely different technique, so I'm genuinely excited to learn new skills and do the best I can.

'Luckily, the first week no one gets eliminated, so I'm excited to go out there and enjoy the vibe. On week two, I'll probably be more nervous. But I'm focused, genuinely, on just getting on the dance floor and enjoying the moment.'

Layton's favourite week is Halloween and he's hoping to get far enough for the fright-night fun, so he can enjoy the 'crazy costumes'. He's also looking forward to delving into the show's glittering wardrobe every week to fully embrace the glitz and glamour.

'The costumes on *Strictly* are unreal,' he says. 'As actors, we are used to putting on costumes and crazy things, so I'm really excited to be myself and perform on *Strictly*. Why wouldn't I be? I'm ready to be *Strictly*-fied.

'I'm absolutely buzzing to be taking part in one of the most iconic shows in the UK and so excited to learn from the best. It's time to bring it to the ballroom and bring on the sequins ... ALL the sequins!'

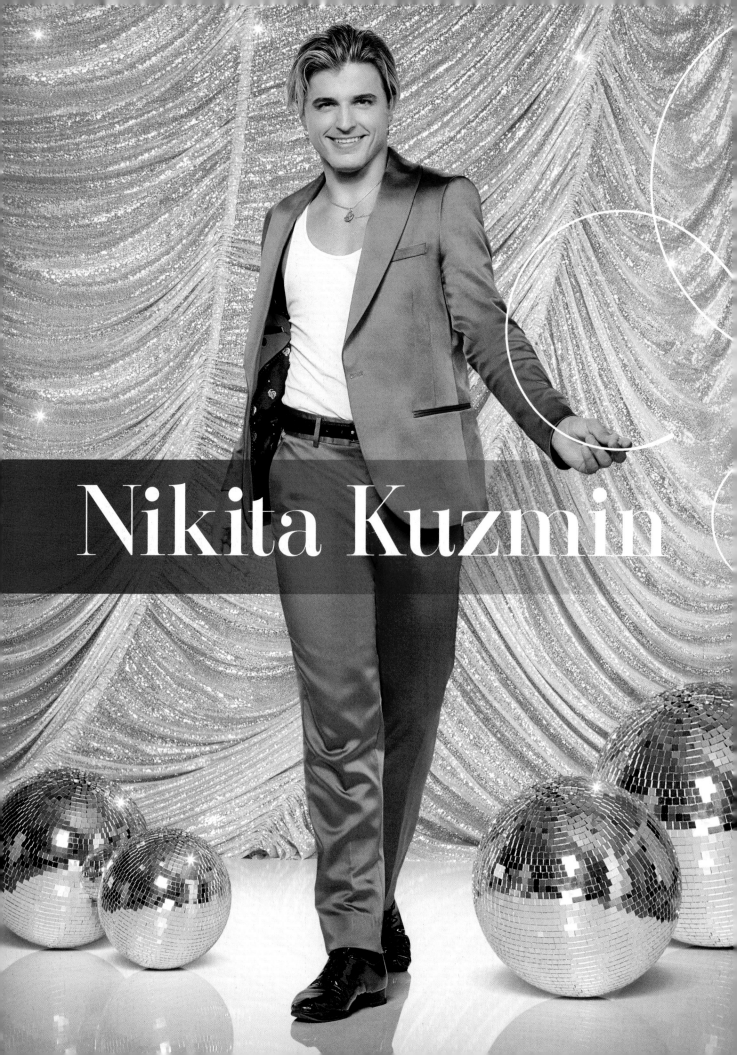

Nikita Kuzmin

It could be third time lucky for Nikita as he takes to the *Strictly* stage with West End star Layton Williams. The *Bad Education* actor is proving to be a perfect pupil.

'Training is going better than I expected,' says Nikita. 'There is a lovely atmosphere in the room and Layton is picking up every single point that I'm telling him, and really listening to me. We've been trying to get the technique and choreography down and, when he has that, we can put a bit more of Layton in every move.

'Our first dance was the Samba, which works really well on his body and his style. It's a hard dance and requires a lot of coordination because the movement is ridiculous, but I've always dreamt of starting on a Samba. There have been so many iconic Sambas on *Strictly*, which I hope we come close to. We are having the most wonderful time, every single day so far, and he's really keen, so he is giving me everything a teacher would like to have in terms of a student.'

With musicals including *Rent* and *Everybody's Talking About Jamie* under his belt, Layton has some moves, but Nikita says he is still on page one when it comes to Latin and ballroom.

'This is so different to what he's been doing before,' he says. 'From every single point, from the feet, ankles and toes to your centre, your spine, coordination and hips, it's completely new. Also, he has never danced in a couple.'

Dancing with his first male celebrity means Nikita can branch out to new areas in his choreography and even switch leads.

'I'm really looking forward to that,' he says. 'Layton has to learn a lot more and get to know the dances before we switch roles, but I am excited to do that somewhere further into the series.'

Nikita was just four when he started dancing in his native Ukraine. He continued to learn ballroom and Latin after his family moved to Italy, when he was nine, and was crowned National Champion six times. At 18, he moved to Germany. He became a professional dancer on the show *Let's Dance* before joining *Strictly* in series 19, partnering Tilly Ramsay. Last year, he danced with Paralympian gold medallist Ellie Simmonds.

'Ellie was fantastic,' he says. 'Choreographing for her was a high point of my career because of how she was with me in the studio, how beautiful a relationship we had. Ellie is so lovely, funny and bubbly. I've been really lucky with every single partner I've had.'

The pair were eliminated in week seven, but Nikita has fond memories of their dances together – and the *Strictly Come Dancing Live Tour*.

As he enters his third series, Nikita is determined to live life in the moment and not with an eye on the Grand Final.

'Everybody has the potential to go all the way, but we're not thinking so far ahead,' he says. 'I'm just giving Layton time to enjoy the dance and not think about next week. I'm telling him to enjoy the small details, enjoy learning something you've never done before and above all, enjoy the dance.'

Strictly for the Record

Taking home the Glitterball trophy may be the ultimate prize, but there are many other amazing firsts both our *Strictly Come Dancing* stars and professionals have achieved along the way. So let's celebrate the show's amazing record-breakers and high-achievers.

Challenge Champ

Every year, the dancers battle it out in the *It Takes Two* Pro Challenge, which sees them take on a different dance step each series and complete as many as possible in 30 seconds. The current champ is Amy Dowden, who earned herself a Guinness World Record for the most back Charleston kick steps, in 2022, with an impressive total of 19.

NADIYA'S DOUBLE WHAMMY

Nadiya Bychkova holds two Guinness World Records after winning the Pro Challenge two years running. In 2020, she danced herself dizzy with the most fleckerls in 30 seconds, with 25 spins. A year later, she was announced as the winner of the challenge again after completing 38 pat-a-cake moves (standing spins with outstretched hand) in 30 seconds.

GIOVANNI'S TWO-STEP

Giovanni Pernice is also a double record-holder, after clinching the title in the Pro Challenge in 2016 and 2017. He took the Guinness World Record for the most Jive kicks and flicks in 30 seconds, with 55, followed by the most Charleston swivel steps, with 24, the year after.

MORE GUINNESS WINNERS

Graziano Di Prima currently holds the world record for most botafogo dance steps in 30 seconds, with 90. Grabbing the title in the 2019 Pro Challenge, he beat the previous record of 79, set by former *Strictly* champ Artem Chigvintsev in 2011.

Oti Mabuse holds the record for the most Jive toe-heel swivel steps in 30 seconds, coming in at 48 in 2018.

The first paired Pro Challenge, in 2014, was won by Karen Hauer and Aljaž Škorjanec, who performed 39 New Yorkers in half a minute.

Kevin Clifton won the prize for the most drunken sailors in 2013, with a whopping 77.

Jill Halfpenny and Darren Bennet, series 2

◀ First Perfect Score

It's not easy to get all four 10 paddles from the discerning judges, and the perfect score has only been awarded 86 times in *Strictly*'s 20 series. In fact, it wasn't awarded until the end of series 2, when winner Jill Halfpenny became the first celebrity to receive a score of 40 for her Grand Final Jive to Elton John's 'I'm Still Standing'.

Ashley Roberts and Pasha Kovalev, series 16

Most Perfect Scores ▶

Series 16 finalist Ashley Roberts received the most 40s in the history of the show with five. She scored her first for her week-nine Jive in Blackpool and followed up with a perfect Semi-final American Smooth before scoring the maximum 120 points for three dances in the Grand Final. Ashley's dance partner, Pasha Kovalev, holds the record for the most perfect scores among the pro dancers, with 13.

Alexandra Burke and Gorka Márquez, series 15

◀ Most 10s

The record for most 10s awarded to one couple throughout a series is shared between Alexandra Burke and Gorka Márquez and Ashley Roberts and Pasha Kovalev, who each earned 32. This is closely followed by Faye Tozer and Giovanni Pernice, with 31, and Rose Ayling-Ellis and Giovanni Pernice with 30.

Rose Ayling-Ellis and Giovanni Pernice, series 19

Earliest 40 ▶

While Craig's 10 paddle is rarely raised before Blackpool week, there have been exceptions. Series-19 champion Rose Ayling-Ellis holds the record for the earliest 40 in the competition, earning her first perfect score in week six for her Tango.

Fleur East and Vito Coppola, series 20

◀ In Pursuit of Perfection

The Rumba has proved the most difficult dance and, as yet, nobody has ever been awarded a perfect score. The perfect Samba proved almost as elusive, but Danny Mac finally broke the spell with a 40 for his series-14 routine with Oti Mabuse. In series 20, Fleur East and Vito Coppola earned the second ever perfect score for their 'Hot Hot Hot' Samba in the Grand Final.

TV Glory ▶

Strictly itself has its own lofty entry in the Guinness World Records, having won the most Best Talent Show gongs at the National Television Awards. It has picked up 11 awards since the category was introduced in 2007, waltzing off with the title in 2008, 2013–14 and 2016–23.

Claudia Winkleman and Tess Daly

National treasure Sir Bruce Forsyth pictured in 2014

◀ Brucie Bonus

The late, great Sir Bruce Forsyth, who presented the show for over a decade, also holds the world record for the longest TV career by a male entertainer, spanning 76 years from 1939 to 2015. He made his TV debut at 11 years old, on a show called *Come and Be Televised*, and went on to host his first show, *Sunday Night at the London Palladium*, from 1958. His final TV appearance was on 13 November 2015, when he co-hosted the Children in Need *Strictly Come Dancing* special.

Annabel Croft

Former tennis pro Annabel is practising a new kind of swing for her turn on the dance floor and is hoping she'll ace the training. And she can't wait for partner Johannes Radebe to show her the secrets behind the magical routines she watches every year.

'I'm so excited to be doing *Strictly*,' she says. 'I have always loved to watch dancing. I could watch dancers all day, but I can't quite figure out how they do what they do because they are so amazing. They all have their own style and it's mesmerising, absolutely joyful. So to be given this opportunity is just amazing. The experience has been so exhilarating already, if a little terrifying at the same time.'

The mum-of-three says her family can't wait to cheer her on from the sidelines – and might even help her practise at home.

'My two daughters are amazing dancers, so I kind of wish they were doing the moves for me!' she laughs. 'They're beyond excited and they've always loved the show, but my son's also excited about coming to watch me in the show, too.'

Born in Kent, Annabel became a British Number One tennis player in her teens and, at 15, was the youngest UK player to compete at Wimbledon for 95 years. She represented Great Britain in prestigious Wightman and Federation Cup competitions and now uses her expertise in her role as a commentator at Wimbledon and a highly respected pundit for major broadcasters including the BBC, Sky, Amazon Prime, ITV and Discovery. Outside of tennis, Annabel has fronted entertainment shows such as *Treasure Hunt* and *Inceptor* and, in 2009, she and her late husband Mel Coleman launched the Annabel Croft Tennis Academy.

A huge fan of the show, she is thrilled to be 'swapping tennis balls for Glitterballs and looking forward to finding some joyfulness in the process'. As a former athlete, she's also determined to throw herself into the training process.

'I love to learn something and then keep trying it again,' she says. 'Even if I keep getting it wrong, I'll keep going with it until I get it right. I'm really looking forward to that and I just hope my brain can keep up with it.

'I want to get to the point where remembering the steps isn't part of it anymore, it's about going with it, with feeling. That will bring me back to my childhood days doing ballet when I was little, which took a back seat when I started tennis. I slightly regret that I didn't keep up ballet because that would have kept me supple!'

Apart from her childhood ballet classes, Annabel has little dance experience but says BBC *Breakfast*'s Sally Nugent taught her how to do the floss dance move at Wimbledon and it's become her signature move.

'It's a bit old-fashioned now, but one day Sally and I were on Centre Court, we were doing an item and we "flossed". I couldn't do it at first, then she taught me and it finally clicked. That's my party trick! It's good to loosen up the hips a bit – I'm always saying that my hips need some oil.'

The ever-stylish pundit has a keen eye for fashion and says dressing up is going to be one of her biggest thrills.

'I can spend hours trawling websites looking at fashion. I've always loved fashion – I love dresses and being feminine, and who wouldn't enjoy putting on those beautiful dresses and the glitter and glam?' she says. 'Also, working with professionals at the top of their field in hair, make-up and costumes ... they are such a major part of this show.'

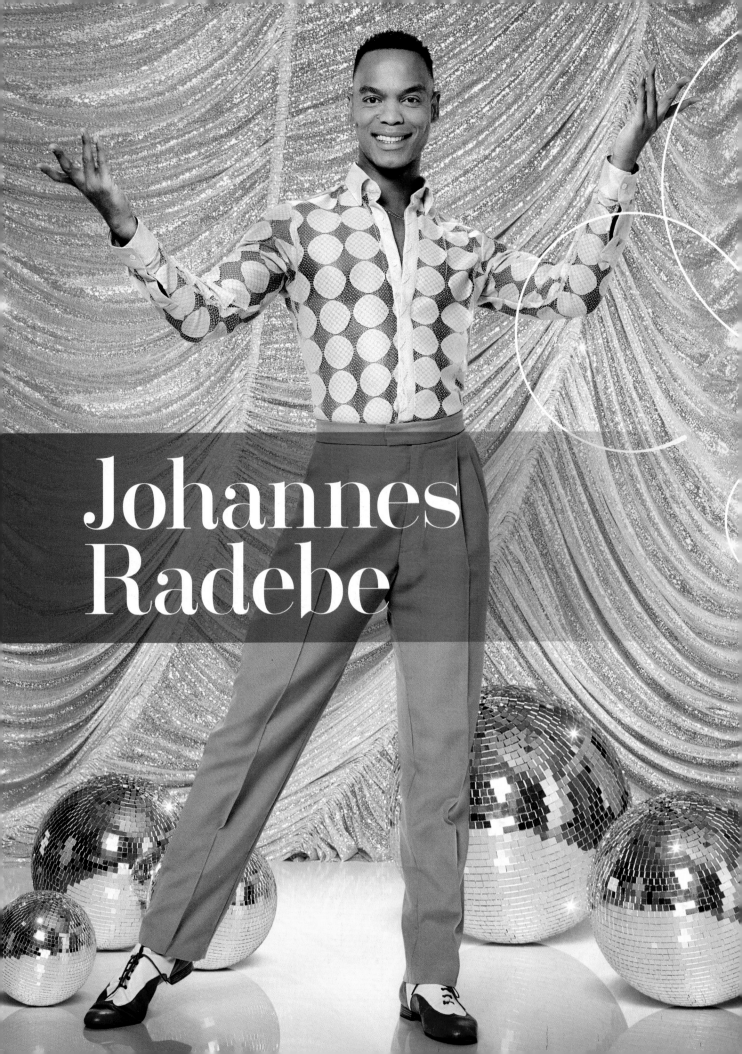

Johannes Radebe

After meeting his series-21 partner, Annabel Croft, on the hallowed turf of Wimbledon's Centre Court, Johannes is full of bounce and ready to have a ball.

'Now that we've been paired together, I can't see how I could be with anyone else,' he says. 'She's a lovely person and somebody I really enjoy spending my time with.

'Annabel is a sportswoman, not a dancer, but she has love for dancing and she wishes she had done it as a child. I told her, "We're doing it for that young girl, so let's live out your best dreams." But she has watched and learned about dance and that comes across. She's got so much potential and I can't wait to discover what she can do.'

What she may lack in dance experience, Annabel is making up for in sheer determination.

'As a teacher you want somebody who's always practising and Annabel is relentless,' says Johannes. 'In the first week, I watched her go to the shop to get lunch, and she was practising her arms as she walked. She practises the choreography every night and when she comes in to training the next day, something has improved. I think her sports background has given her that work ethic, focus and grit.'

Johannes also discovered early on that his latest pupil is fearless when it comes to lifts.

'She's not scared,' he says. 'For the opening of the show, I told her, "I'm going to spin you upside down," and she said, "Okay." That's a beautiful thing because it means I can be a bit more adventurous with my choreography.'

The South African dancer says standing on Wimbledon's Centre Court was a 'surreal' experience.

'I've never had the opportunity to go to Wimbledon and there's an atmosphere about that place, which is down to its history,' he says. 'We volleyed on the court and Annabel said,

"You're a natural," so she saw potential in me as well. We're definitely going to return to the tennis court so she can teach me.'

Johannes began dancing at seven and is two-time Professional South African Latin Champion and three-time South African Amateur Latin Champion. He joined the South African version of *Strictly Come Dancing* in 2014 before moving to the UK show five years ago. Last year, he partnered comedian Ellie Taylor.

'We got on like a house on fire,' he says. 'I've never laughed so much in all my years on *Strictly*. I remember our partnership with great fondness and lots of laughter, and we are still close today.'

The couple's favourite dance was their Halloween routine to the *Hocus Pocus* track "I Put a Spell on You", which saw them both dress as witches.

'It was nice to see Ellie come into her own in that dance,' he says. 'She started finding her feet and her confidence grew. It's beautiful as a teacher to see your student grow.'

As well as looking forward to getting on the dance floor with his latest student, Johannes is excited for the return of the series he loves.

'Once again I'm looking forward to the magic of *Strictly Come Dancing*. I can't wait for the audience at home to see it because I think it is beautiful. The fact that ballroom dancing is such a big part of the nation and has such a reach still blows my mind.

'I'm looking forward to spending time with Annabel and turning her into a beautiful dancer. On the first day of rehearsal, I asked her what she wanted from this experience and she said, "It wouldn't be fair to me to compare myself to anybody. I'm here as a student and I want to learn how to dance."'

Get the Look

Fun, fast and furious, nothing evokes the spirit of the Roaring Twenties like the Charleston. Series-20 contestant Ellie Taylor unleashed her inner flapper girl in a fabulous routine to the Cole Porter classic 'Friendship' with partner Johannes Radebe. Here, Make-up Designer Lisa Armstrong and Hair Designer Lisa Davey reveal how you can achieve the 1920s look with a modern twist, while Head of Wardrobe Vicky Gill creates a simple headdress you can make at home.

ke-up by *Lisa Armstrong*

look we want a nod to the flapper
e keeping it fresh and up-to-date.
t for heavy eyeshadow in matte dark
and black for a full-on smoky eye,
ld red lip for dramatic effect.
art with a primer on the eyelid so
adow sticks. I recommend using a
under-eye sheet mask to keep the
from eyeshadow droppage, too.

2 Next, apply a sweep of dark brown
across the eyelid, past the socket line and
up towards the brow bone, leaving a slight
gap between the brow and the shadow.
Crucially, it must be blended to avoid
harsh blocks of colour.

3 Go over the top with black shadow,
near the socket line and again up towards
the brow. Blend well to create a cool,
playful, sexy look to reflect the cheeky
Charleston.

4 Using a black eyeliner or liquid pen, sweep along the upper lid, keeping as close to the lash line as you can, and add a flick at the end. Then use a black pencil in the waterline on the lower lid and smudge a bit of the brown and black underneath the eye. Add a fluffy false lash on the upper lids for drama, and lots of mascara on the bottom lashes.

5 Comb the brows, then use a powder with an angled brush or a sharp eyebrow pencil, in your natural colour, to define the arch – another nod to the Twenties look.

6 Add a little highlighter on the brow bone, between the brow and the eyeshadow.

7 Once you've perfected your eye make-up, take the under-eye mask off and use micellar water or a wipe to clean the skin of any make-up droppage and excess oil from the eye mask.

8 Apply concealer and foundation to the face, keeping it clean and fresh.

9 Add highlighter to the cheekbone, then add a pop of rosy-pink blush to give it that playful, fresh-faced look, as if someone has pinched the cheeks.

10 Use a sharpened cherry-red lip liner to accentuate the bow of the lip, then bring the pencil down to the outer corner of the mouth and sweep along the bottom lipline. Use highlighter again in the dip of the bow of the lip to make it pop.

11 Fill in with red lipstick using a lip brush. If you're rocking a red lip with such a heavy eye, it needs to be precise, so go around the outside with a cotton bud dipped in micellar water to tidy up the edges, then, with the other end of the bud, apply concealer to sharpen the shape.

12 Finish with powder across the T-zone, under the eye, around the nose and on the chin. Give that a minute to set, then spritz with a fixing spray.

Hair by Lisa Davey

The Twenties look is a classic bob or a finger wave, so the style we created for Ellie is a soft, glamorous wave, between a Hollywood wave and a Marcel wave. It is a simple style to achieve at home, using heated tongs and section clips. Because of time factors on the show, we start with dry hair.

1 First, spray the hair with a setting product.

2 Starting at the front, take a small section of hair, then wrap it round a small heated tong, all the way from the bottom to the top. Release after five to eight seconds.

3 Repeat on the next section, then the next, all around the head, working in one direction.

4 Brush the hair. You should get a flowing wave all the way through.

5 Add section clips along the dip of each wave and set with hairspray.

6 If setting early, leave the section clips in place until you are ready, then spray with hairspray before removing.

7 Add any hair jewellery or a headband (see below) and then generously spray once again.

Headband by Vicky Gill

To achieve a similar look to Ellie's Charleston headband, keep it simple by using a braid. There are lots of haberdashery options to choose from, which you can find in shops or online. They range from stretch metallic elastics to guipure lace, which is a little more expensive. There are also upholstery braids, sequin braids and beading. The braid can be embellished if you like, and for the fastening options, you can use a hook and bar or a swimwear fastener or create a loop with the braid to slide a kirby grip into the hair.

1 Measure the circumference of your head, then add 4–8cm to the total measurement to accommodate a fastener. Cut the braid to the required length.

2 Thread each end of the braid through the two components of the fastener, if using, and fold back the excess braid on the inside of the band, sewing down to create a loop.

3 For more security you can stitch ribbon onto the inside of the headband, creating gaps in the stitching at intervals to slide more kirby grips through, if required.

Apply the rhinestones using PVA glue

4 To embellish, choose rhinestones in the colours that work with your outfit. We used a large (size ss30) rhinestone through the middle with a smaller one (ss16) either side, sitting the smaller ones in the gaps.

5 Dot the material with PVA glue, then use a pencil with beeswax on the end to help you pick up the gems and position them on the glue dots. Allow to dry before wearing.

Fold back and sew the extra braid to create a loop for a kirby grip or fastener

Former Latin champ Motsi returned to her first love on this year's launch show, dancing up a storm with the rest of the judges and the professional dancers in a spectacular group number, and she loved every minute.

'It's always fun to dance and I miss dancing,' she says. 'I don't dance as much as I would like to these days. It was fun to put the dancing shoes back on, challenge myself and feel those vibes again.'

Going into her fifth series on the panel, the South African judge says she also enjoyed meeting the new celebrities, as she does each year.

'The launch show is about meeting everybody and I think we've got some great personalities this year,' she says. 'There's going to be some great dancing, that's for sure, but I also feel like we have people who are very positive, who are looking forward to doing Strictly and who bring in bundles of personality, fun and presence. They're all very enthusiastic, and every generation is covered in this cast, which is great.'

Motsi, who was a pro dancer on Let's Dance in Germany before joining the German show's judging panel in 2007, has plenty of advice for the new recruits and says the key to success is gaining as much knowledge as you can early on.

'At the beginning, make sure you concentrate, take in as much as you can, and it will get easier as you go,' she says. 'That's when you are most receptive to learning something new, so get to grips with the technical work and the fundamentals.'

When it comes to what makes a Strictly champion, Motsi looks for specific qualities but says it's not always the celebrities she picks out on day one.

'To be a Strictly champion, first of all, you must be able to transmit whatever you are feeling on the dance floor to the audience,' she says. 'The audience need to connect with you. Secondly, I think it's a combination of beautiful dancing, a great personality chemistry and improving each week.'

Last series, Motsi remembers the moment when winner Hamza Yassin took her breath away and proved he was a serious contender for the Glitterball trophy.

'I loved Hamza's Salsa in week four,' she says. 'I think [he] was the winner because his personality was humble and he was always learning, always improving.

'Last year's Final was very interesting. I love a Final that is so harmonious. You had beautiful dancing, you had Hamza, you had Samba queen Fleur East, you had a very technical Molly Rainford and a wonderful story in Helen Skelton.'

This year, Motsi is eager to get to know the new Strictly stars and make some more unforgettable memories.

'I'm looking forward to learning about new people and being back with all the other judges, because we get along so well,' she says. 'But most of all, it's about those great shows, those fun moments and those happy moments. I'm looking forward to that.'

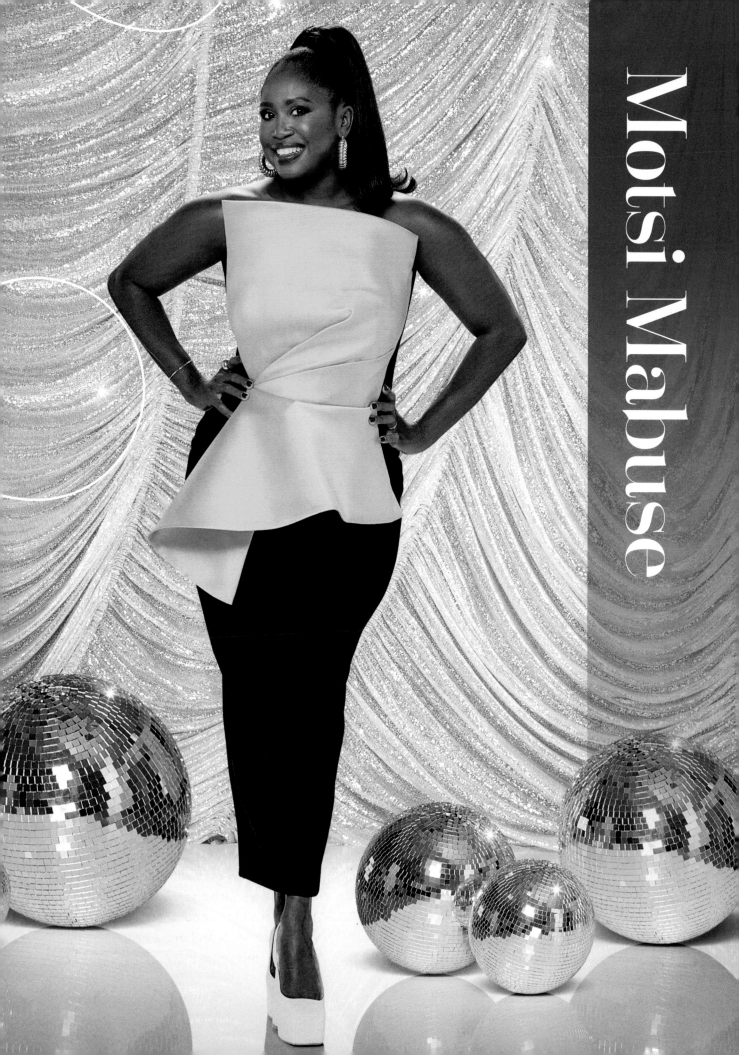

Motsi Mabuse

Strictly Word Search

Can you seek out the answers to our *Strictly*-themed word search, following our handy clues?

Clues

- Fast-paced dance associated with flappers in the 1920s
- Pro who lifted the Glitterball trophy in series 20 (first name only)
- Perfect score
- Last name of pro Neil
- Pro who partnered John Whaite in the series-19 Final
- Ms Winkleman
- *Strictly*'s longest-serving pro
- Anton's surname
- The four experts on the panel
- Head judge's first name
- Series-20 finalist, partnered by Vito Coppola
- *Strictly* presenter
- Latin party dance
- Series-20 finalist Helen
- Energetic Latin dance with lots of flicks and kicks
- Surname of dancer Luba

J	W	O	A	T	I	W	O	J	P	L	Y	X	B	C
F	O	R	T	Y	C	R	A	O	D	G	Y	H	U	J
Z	C	L	E	K	A	R	E	N	H	A	U	E	R	O
C	O	T	M	F	Z	R	P	E	C	O	R	S	L	H
H	D	A	L	U	P	Y	W	S	I	M	D	U	G	A
A	K	S	N	E	S	H	I	R	L	E	Y	Q	J	N
R	H	N	O	O	R	H	C	L	A	U	D	I	A	N
L	D	G	E	K	T	X	T	E	S	M	V	B	L	E
E	C	J	O	H	F	L	E	U	R	E	A	S	T	S
S	P	P	J	Y	Z	T	E	S	K	C	H	A	R	R
T	X	D	U	B	E	K	E	K	N	Z	T	A	W	A
O	E	U	D	F	W	I	P	A	S	L	A	S	Q	D
N	H	I	G	Z	C	H	A	R	D	C	K	B	J	E
N	N	P	E	E	T	E	S	S	D	A	L	Y	L	B
S	C	I	S	G	H	M	D	A	K	K	U	S	H	E

Back at the helm of *It Takes Two* for the third year, Janette is delighted that pal Fleur East will be joining her as co-presenter this year.

'I love Fleur and we get along really well,' she says. 'During the series, I only see the celebrities when they come and chat with me on *It Takes Two* and if I pop in to the studio, so I don't get to socialise as much as I used to. But when I host the *Strictly Come Dancing Live Tour*, I get to spend more time with them all, and Fleur and I really hit it off. She's so much fun, hilarious and quirky.'

The teaming of a former *Strictly* professional dancer with a celebrity finalist means both presenters have a unique perspective on the couples' experience, and Janette believes Fleur's time on the show puts her on the ideal footing for her new role.

'Fleur was the perfect call to host *It Takes Two* with me because she's walked in those shoes and was there all the way to the end,' she says. 'She understands what the celebs are going through and knows what she's talking about. She was one of the best in the series, danced so many iconic numbers and got so many 40s. She'll definitely be a good ear for every couple that comes on to the show.'

Janette, who danced on *Strictly* for eight series before taking on the spin-off show, had an expert eye on the professionals last year and loved what she saw.

'The last series was amazing and we had some awesome new pros,' she says. 'Vito and Carlos made the Final in their first year and it was Jowita's first time with a celebrity partner and she lifted the trophy. All of them were incredible to watch in the Final, and Gorka and Helen were amazing together as well. Every year it just gets better and better.'

With an impressive line-up for series 21, Janette is anticipating another incredible year.

'What makes it so special is the fact that you've got every age, from baby-faced Bobby Brazier to Angela Rippon who's about to turn 79, but I reckon they'll both be competing neck and neck with each other. That's the beauty of the show. You get something for everyone and everyone just brings something fabulous to the table.

'I always love finding the dark horses, like Hamza, who won the series [last year]. With him we didn't know what to expect but he came out and danced that Foxtrot in week one and you got a glimpse of what was there, then he did a fabulous Salsa and went on to win. I'm looking forward to seeing who the dark horse will be in this group.'

Janette – who will host *It Takes Two* on Wednesdays, Thursdays and alternate Fridays – says she can't wait to interview the class of 2023 on the show.

'I'm looking forward to meeting the celebrities, getting to know them and experience their journey with them,' she says. 'I always loved watching my celebrity partner grow on *Strictly*. Seeing what they looked like on Monday to what they delivered on Saturday night always made me feel proud. I don't get to do that with a celebrity any more, but when they come and chat with me, I feel a little of that journey with them and I can watch them develop and be there for their ups and downs.'

The bubbly host is delighted to be returning to the show this year and says it remains her 'dream job'.

'Besides dancing on *Strictly*, it's the best job I've ever had,' she says. 'I'm still dancing on tour, but I always said when I hung up my dance shoes, I would love to do a show like *It Takes Two*, which celebrates dancing – something I'm so passionate about. To be able to host *ITT* and still be part of the *Strictly* family is amazing.'

Janette Manrara

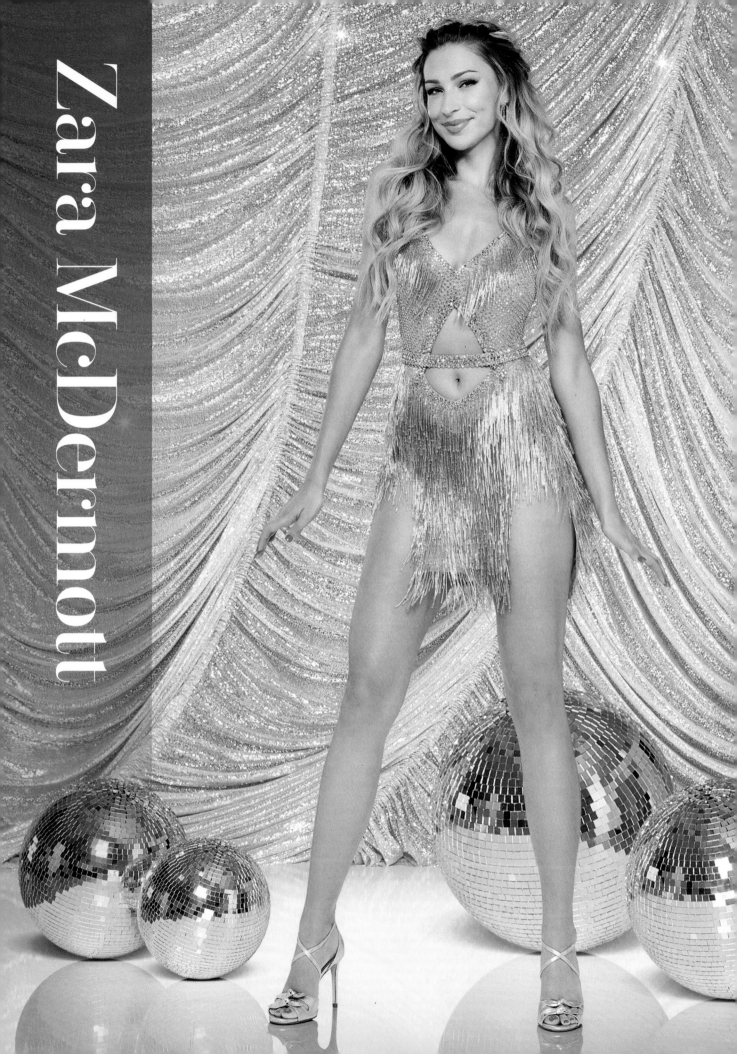

Zara McDermott

Documentary-maker Zara has always been a fan of *Strictly* and didn't have to think twice when she was asked to take part.

'I've watched the show since I was seven years old, so this is like a dream for me,' she says. 'It honestly took me months to get my head round the fact I was actually doing it, and it still didn't feel real until the first meeting with the other celebrities. We rehearsed how we would walk out on the show, and when my name was announced I literally wanted to cry. I am so grateful to be here.'

Although she is not nervous about the dancing, Zara says seeing her family in the *Strictly* studio, beaming with pride, might shake her.

'I'm honestly feeling nervous about that moment of seeing my parents and my grandparents in the audience and trying to hold it together,' she says. 'It's going to be the best moment of my life seeing them there, and how proud they are of me, because I'm not just doing it for me, I'm also doing it for them.'

While her family are cheering her on, there's one special *Strictly* superfan who will be in her heart throughout the competition.

'I watched the first series with my nan and we used to dance around our living room trying to learn all the dances together. She's sadly passed away now, but she would be over the moon if she knew that I was doing this. I feel like she's looking down on me, and I'm thinking of her a lot with every moment of this. She's my guardian angel, watching and being really proud.'

Born in East London, Zara worked in the civil service before appearing on *Love Island* in 2018 and going on to star in *Made in Chelsea*. She now fronts hard-hitting documentaries on the BBC, tackling issues that affect young people today.

'I'm already doing my dream job, which I love, so *Strictly* is an experience and an opportunity for me to learn a new skill that I would never otherwise have done,' she says. 'The idea of pushing myself out of my comfort zone is something that I've tried to do the whole of my twenties. Dancing is something that I know I'm not very good at. I've never been the girl to dance in a nightclub because I'm really nervous about how I look and so this is going to be throwing myself into the deep end, doing something that I'm absolutely not confident with, and just giving it a go.'

Paired with Graziano Di Prima, Zara says she is keen to get everything just right. 'My biggest challenge will be trying not to get annoyed at myself if I get something wrong and remembering it's okay not to be good at it in the first few days. Dancing with a pro like Graziano, I'm going to feel like I want to be at that level, so I need to keep reminding myself my job is to just do my best. If I'm not good at something, I get quite frustrated, so it's about being kind to myself.'

With happy memories of being dazzled by the *Strictly* dresses when she first watched the show at seven, she is excited to be embracing the sparkle for herself this year.

'My job, making documentaries, is the complete opposite of glam,' she says. 'It's just you and a tiny team and there's no hair and make-up; it's all do-it-yourself. So giving rein to other people to do hair, make-up, and to glitz and glam you up for the show is living the dream. I am absolutely buzzing about the costumes. It's going to be incredible.'

Graziano
Di Prima

Having put three radio and TV presenters through their paces already, Graziano is raring to go with documentary-maker Zara McDermott – and is already bowled over by her enthusiasm.

'Zara is the humblest, sweetest person,' he says. 'She has everything to learn about dancing, but she is determined to put in her all and be the best she possibly can. She said she was so happy to be partnered with me. Every dance is going to be completely new to her, but she is a massive fan of the show, and has been watching since she was seven with her grandparents. Also, her mum is a huge fan of *Strictly* and of me. After we were paired, we called Zara's mum and she was literally screaming.

'I'm very, very happy to be paired with Zara and I'm going to do my best to help her learn how to dance.'

The Sicilian dancer says his celebrity partner is a diligent pupil, but it's too early to predict how far they can go as a partnership.

'It's not about the Final,' he says. 'I see the journey and I'm going to take it day by day. Each person is different, each person has different dance skills, and every year we're starting with a new page. With Zara, we are starting from the basics, and we'll see where we go.'

Dancing from the age of six, Graziano moved to Bologna to compete at 17, becoming Italian Latin champion. He joined *Strictly* in 2018, dancing with DJ Vick Hope. In series 20 he made the Quarter-final with actress and presenter Kym Marsh.

'Kym and I really connected and she is still a close friend,' he says. 'She was incredible because she was filming until 3 p.m. on *Waterloo Road*, and then rehearsing and still producing amazing dances. I couldn't be happier with what we achieved.'

As he enters his sixth series, Graziano couldn't be more revved up.

'I can't wait to be back because since I joined *Strictly*, my life has changed completely,' he says. 'I feel I've been part of the show for long enough that I can fully appreciate the beauty of it and not overthink it. I'm enjoying it more each year, because you learn more, you think about the judges' advice and you find ways to make it better, each step of the way. "Make it work" is my mantra because, at the start, you don't know the person in front of you, you don't know the other couples' dances, so it's like taking a big jump and then finding a way to land.'

Graziano describes his teaching method as 'sweet and sour', joking, 'I'll say, "That's beautiful, so proud of you. Do it again."' But his only goal is to make sure his celebrity partner has a blast.

'First of all, I want to connect with a friend, because when you make a friend there is trust and you can build a relationship that will take you through the series,' he says. 'As a professional dancer, I am very competitive, but the main thing is that my partner is going to enjoy the series. They have just one chance to do *Strictly* and I want to be the person who's going to bring them through, make them feel like they loved every second and learned to dance. That's my goal, every series.'

Global Dance Party

Dance is a universal language, and nothing proves that more than the global success of the *Strictly Come Dancing* franchise. Since the show launched in the UK in 2004, the format – known internationally as *Dancing with the Stars* – has become the BBC's most successful export and a licence for the format has been sold to 61 countries around the world, including China, Japan and India. Latvia is the latest to join the party, launching their show in 2022.

Let's take a quick twirl around the world.

Australia

The first country to adopt the format, Australia launched *Dancing with the Stars* just months after the first *Strictly* aired in the UK, in 2004. Now in its twentieth series, the show's judges have included Aussie expert Craig Revel Horwood, in series 16 and 17, and former *Strictly* pro Tristan MacManus.

Guest judges have included Pamela Anderson, Olivia Newton-John and Dame Edna Everage, and Hollywood star Chris Hemsworth appeared as a contestant. One of the most iconic moments from the show came in 2019, when drag star Courtney Act danced a powerful Tango, telling the story of their awakening to gender fluidity.

Germany

Let's Dance launched on German TV in April 2006 and completed its sixteenth series in 2023. UK judge Motsi Mabuse has been on the judging panel since the fourth series and Oti Mabuse competed in two series, dancing with singer Daniel Küblböck and TV presenter Niels Ruf. In 2020, Nikita Kuzmin was partnered with rapper Sabrina Setlur on the show.

 ## Ireland

Strictly pro Kai Widdrington danced for four years on Ireland's *Dancing with the Stars*, and was a finalist twice, with sports personality Anna Geary in 2018, and Miss Universe Ireland Grainne Gallanagh in 2020. *Derry Girls* actor Leah O'Rourke was among the celebrities to take part in series 6, in 2023, which was won by radio presenter Carl Mullan.

 ## Italy

Ballando con le Stelle first aired in January 2005 and has been essential Saturday-night viewing for Italian audiences ever since, with up to 4.6 million tuning in. The 2021 champion was *Strictly* pro Vito Coppola, dancing with pop star Arisa. Bianca Gascoigne was runner-up, with Italian dancer Simone Di Pasquale. Nikita's older sister, Anastasia Kuzmina, has also appeared as a professional dancer on the show.

 ## Poland

Kicking off in 2005, Poland's *Taniec z Gwiazdami* has had the most series outside the US, with 2023 seeing the twenty-sixth series. The judging panel is composed of retired professional dancer Iwona Szymańska-Pavlović, dancer Michał Malitowski, singer Andrzej Piaseczny, and actor and comedian Andrzej Grabowski.

 ## USA

With 31 series under its sparkly belt, the US *Dancing with the Stars* is the most prolific of the international shows and the recipient of four Emmy Awards. Len Goodman was head judge from the show's launch in 2005 until his final appearance in November 2022, alongside fellow judges Carrie Ann Inaba and Bruno Tonioli. The current judge lineup includes professional Latin and ballroom dancer Derek Hough. Winners include Donny Osmond and Nicole Scherzinger, and former contestants include Jerry Springer, David Hasselhoff, Buzz Aldrin, Pamela Anderson and tennis legend Martina Navratilova. The series-31 champion was TikTok star Charli D'Amelio dancing with pro Mark Ballas, son of *Strictly* head judge Shirley.

Fun Facts

- *Dancing with the Stars* has been produced in every continent on earth except Antarctica.

- Globally, the show has won almost 70 awards. By March 2023, there had been over 460 series and over 5,500 episodes worldwide.

- In Ukraine, the winner of the 2006 series was future president Volodymyr Zelenskyy.

- The spin-off, *DWTS: Juniors*, has run in four territories, the latest being Germany in 2021.

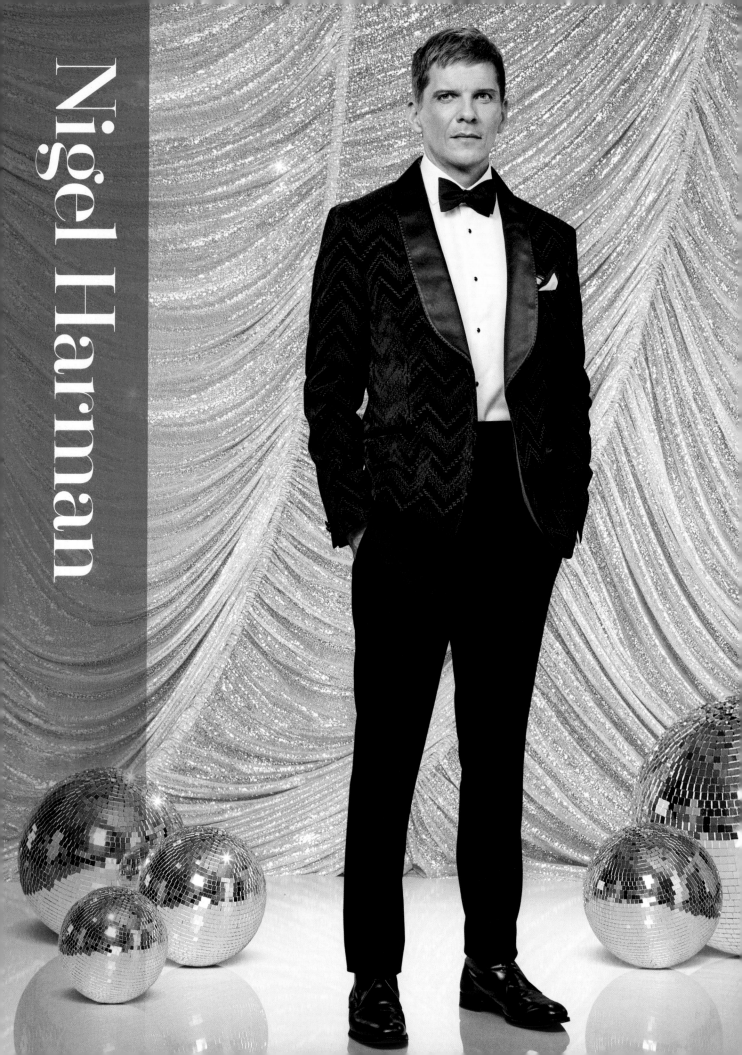

Nigel Harman

Casualty star Nigel is swapping his scrubs for sparkle as he prepares to wow on the dance floor. But he admits his ballroom and Latin skills might need some nursing.

'I am used to live theatre and I haven't been this nervous for some time, but in a really good way, because I'm also very excited. I can't wait,' he says. 'There's a line in *Top Gun*, which is, "Your ego's writing cheques your body can't cash," and that's how I feel. My head is saying, "You're going to be a really good dancer," and then you watch something back and you think, "What? It looks like that? Because it feels like this!" There's a discrepancy there and I'm hoping the two will get to meet at some point.'

Born in Surrey, Nigel was introduced to amateur dramatics by his parents and went professional at eight, with a role in *Tenko*, and the comedy series *Alas Smith and Jones*. He went on to join the original West End cast of *Mamma Mia!* before becoming a household name when he landed the role of Dennis Rickman in *EastEnders*. He has trodden the boards in numerous theatre shows, including *Guys and Dolls* opposite Sarah Lancashire, *A Chorus of Disapproval* and *Shrek the Musical*, which he also directed.

Nigel, who is partnering Katya Jones, is hoping his musical-theatre experience will help him on the dance floor, but he says the disciplines are very different – even down to the facial expressions.

'I'm hoping that on the *Strictly* dance floor it will all come together.'

In the run-up to his stint on the show, Nigel has been seeking advice from *Casualty* co-star Charles Venn, who danced with *Strictly* pro Karen Hauer in 2018.

'Charles gave me two bits of advice,' he says. 'One was, "Be yourself and let whatever happens happen." He also said to me, "Cardio, cardio cardio." Charles is superfit, much fitter than me, but he said, "I was absolutely shattered," and if he's saying that, I don't know what that says for me.'

Nigel, who has recently qualified as a meditation teacher, has also been trying to fit in a little extra fitness training before the show – with mixed results.

'I fully intended to prepare and I did go back to the gym, so that was good,' he says. 'Then I felt the big fitness push was going to come over this summer when I was in France, but I ended up relaxing a bit too much and eating baguettes, so I'm slightly behind where I wanted to be.'

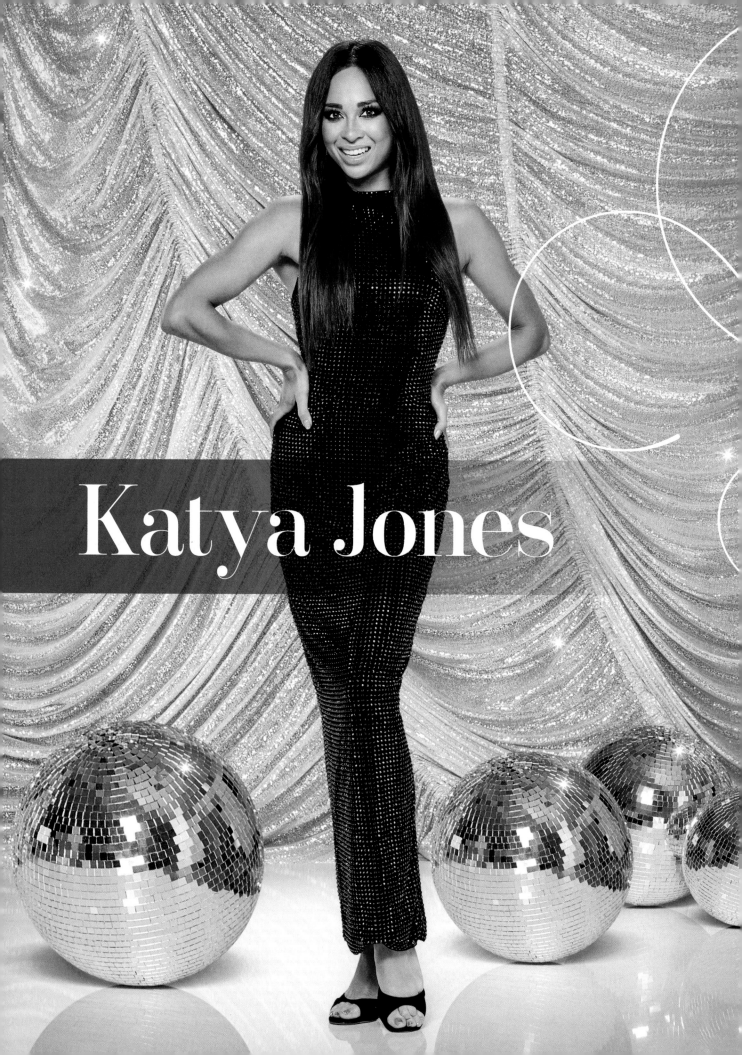

Katya Jones

Having danced with sports personalities for the last three series, former champ Katya – who won series 15 with Joe McFadden – is hoping new partner Nigel Harman's acting skills will come in handy.

'Regardless of their occupation, every person is different, their personalities are different, and that's what I love about *Strictly*,' she says. While Nigel has trodden many a board on the West End stage, Katya says he will be starting from scratch in the rehearsal room.

'Nigel loves a live audience and he was confident going into the first group dance, but nobody is ready for the wildness and excitement of the *Strictly* audience,' she says. 'Halfway through, he looked at me and went, "It is a lot, isn't it?" There's definitely a sense of the unknown.'

Katya and her new partner hit it off immediately and, she says, on their first meeting, 'We put each other at ease. We've got good banter going on and I feel really comfortable in his presence. He's a very caring person and gets excited for other people if they do something well, which is lovely. But I can feel there's a little fire in his belly, which is great.'

Katya is looking forward to putting her new pupil through his paces in both Latin and ballroom but thinks he'll be an 'all-rounder'.

'He likes the physicality of the Latin, but I have a feeling he might be good at ballroom, because he's got the stature and posture. I'm excited to find out, because it doesn't always turn out the way that you think it will.'

While Nigel has starred in musicals, including *Shrek* and *Guys and Dolls*, the seasoned pro has not decided whether to draw on her pupil's past characters. 'The truth is, you can't plan anything,' she says. 'The routines just come naturally or organically when you start to dance with your celebrity partner and spend time with each other. Also, they grow throughout the competition. You can't plan magic!'

Born in St Petersburg, Katya is three-time World Amateur Latin champion and four times undefeated British National Professional champion. She made a memorable *Strictly* debut in series 14 with Ed Balls and won the Grand Final with Joe McFadden a year later. Last year, she created more unforgettable moments with former footballer Tony Adams.

'Tony is a legend and he's taken away so much from it,' she says. 'We don't remember what scores we got for any of the numbers, but we remember all the laughter we had and the friendship we took away from it. And hopefully the audience will remember the Tony Adams special, when he stripped off in the Samba!'

Her favourite dance of the series was the couple's Quickstep, to 'The Devil Went Down to Georgia', in Halloween week.

'That was a breakthrough for both of us,' she says. 'Anton commented that Tony was a proper dancer now and that's the moment he realised he can really do it and the effort he'd been putting in for weeks was really worth it. That was a special moment.'

As the new series dawns, Katya is ready to wow *Strictly* fans once again.

'I'm looking forward to creating more magic and entertaining the nation, but also creating special moments for Nigel and his family, because they are big fans of the show,' she says. 'They gather together on Saturday and Sunday nights to watch it, so it's something that brings the whole family together, and his daughter is beyond thrilled he's joined the cast. So it's about creating those moments that they will treasure forever as a family, as well as sharing my love for dance with someone else and gaining a new friend.'

Returning to the judges' panel for the third year, Anton has been casting an eye over the latest *Strictly* stars and says the wide range of personalities on this year's show means the nation will get behind their favourites.

'As always, there are some very familiar faces and some that I don't know so well, but after the launch show, we're already rooting for all of them,' he says. 'It's a great combination and a lovely bunch, and they've done a great job of partnering them up, so we're in for a great series.'

The former *Strictly* professional, who competed on the ballroom circuit before joining the show, is thrilled that former *Come Dancing* host Angela Rippon is joining the cast this year.

'It's terrific that Angela's on the show,' he says. 'Angela is woven into the fabric of *Come Dancing* and ballroom dancing in the UK. She's synonymous with it, so I suppose it is a surprise to us all that she's never done it before. She is an absolute legend of broadcasting, so we're all excited to see her dance. Plus, at 78, she's an inspiration to people of a certain age who want to get up and have a go.

'I've partnered women in their seventies on the show, including Lesley Joseph, who was wonderful, and there's no reason why you shouldn't be able to dance at that age.'

Having taught celebrity partners for the first 18 series of *Strictly Come Dancing*, Anton has a unique insight into the way the new recruits will be feeling as they first take to the dance floor.

When they're in the room for the first time and they're dancing the group dance on the dance floor, the feeling is not to be underestimated. It's an extraordinary thing, to walk onto that *Strictly Come Dancing* dance floor with everybody else and to be part of the show. Also, you're watching the professionals dance in a group number and, at this year's launch show, the judges did

a brilliant number as well, if I do say so myself. Those routines could be intimidating but also hugely inspirational.'

The former ballroom champ says the new line-up shows incredible promise and he's hoping for a series that packs as much punch as last year, when the highly contested Final boasted four incredible dancers in Fleur East, Helen Skelton, Molly Rainford and winner Hamza Yassin.

'Last year was a classic, one of the best ever,' he says. 'I remember thinking, not long into the series, that this was remarkable because the standard was so good, so quickly. Even before Blackpool, we were in a position where there were eight couples left and any four of them could have made the Final. It was one of those situations where every week we had to lose somebody great, who could have potentially won it. It was an extraordinary standard.'

Knowing how much it means to get to the Final, Anton says it was amazing to see three new professional dancers make the Grand Final.

'It takes a bit of time to develop and learn, so it's not always easy for the newer pros,' he says. 'So for Vito and Carlos to go straight in and Jowita to win with her first celebrity was incredible.'

Anton is thrilled to be returning as a judge again this year and is looking forward to seeing the celebrities improve week by week. And he does admit to the odd tinge of envy as he watches the incredible routines each week.

'Sometimes there are numbers, like Helen and Gorka's "Mein Herr" dance last year, that make me think, "Wow! I'd love to have done that number." Also when Hamza did "New York, New York" I got a tinge of jealousy,' he laughs. 'But there are many, many numbers where I think, "I'm glad I'm sitting here."'

Anton Du Beke

Choreography Corner

From the spectacular opening numbers to the couples' dances, each *Strictly* weekend involves extensive and ground-breaking choreography with up to 18 routines a week. Overseeing every step is *Strictly*'s very own Lord of the Dance, Creative Director Jason Gilkison, who not only choreographs many of the group numbers and comes up with ideas and concepts throughout the series, but also helps guide the pros in their own routines.

Jason, who was undefeated Australian Latin Champion from 1981 to 1997, begins working on the new series as early as May, getting together with a core team, including Executive Producer Sarah James, Series Editor Jack Gledhill and Music Producer Ian Masterson, to discuss the structure of the show.

'The first month is preparing the look of the entire series, which means working out if there is a special celebration, such as last year's BBC centenary or the anniversary of James Bond, that we want to mark and which week of the series Halloween falls in, when we're going to Blackpool, ideas for Movie Week and so on.

'Once we have the structure, we start looking at group dances and thinking about new outside choreographers we could bring in. We have regulars we love working with, such as Elizabeth Honan and Matt Flint, but we also interview new choreographers to see if they're a good fit. It's about the heart and soul of the show, which is the Latin and ballroom dances, and thinking how we can use the group dances to take them a step further, whether that's a big Argentine Tango number, a Quickstep or a Lindy Hop. We bring in experts to work with the pros and take that dance to the next level.'

Rehearsals on the group dances begin in August and, once the celebrities are signed up, the process of pairing them with the pro partners begins.

'I come in from a technical point of view, so, for example, looking at the couple's heights,' says Jason. 'Also, we take into consideration the pros and their teaching styles. Finally, you can't overlook chemistry. Ideally, we get the celebrities in a room and do "speed dancing", where they dance with each pro for 20 seconds and move on, so we can see how they work together.'

Once the live shows get underway, Jason and the team are working three to four weeks in advance, as well as thinking about the current week. He talks us through a typical week during the run of the series.

Sunday

The pros usually start working on next week's routine, so myself and my assistant choreographers, Ash-Leigh Hunter and Arduino Bertoncello, are on board to get into their heads, particularly if they were in the bottom two the night before. A lot of talking and planning happens on Sunday because by Monday, when the celebrities are in rehearsal, the routine has to take shape.

Monday to Wednesday

The pros have a meeting with us each week to discuss how everything's going, if there's anything they are worried about and plans for the following week. For example, if they need to commission a prop that takes a while to build.

Every pro with a celebrity has at least one drop-in from me per week. Some like their visit early on so they can get my opinion up front, while they're putting the routine together. Others prefer me to visit on a Wednesday when the

you change?' They also send me a video of the routine, and I'll give them comments, like, 'That move might push your celebrity too far,' etc.

Occasionally, if the pro wants help to work something out, they work with one of the assistants. Arduino and Ash-Leigh have worked with me for years. The main thing is that the pros feel supported because they have so much on their plate.

On Monday morning, between 8.30am and midday, we may also be rehearsing the group number and the pro dance for the music act. With couples rehearsing all over the country, putting it all together in those first few days becomes a massive jigsaw puzzle.

Thursday

The heads of department have meetings, but my assistants and I can take a step back because the couples' routines need to be over the line by Wednesday night. This means that by Saturday, the routine feels like an old friend

Friday

Friday is a big day, with everything coming together in the studio and the couples seeing each other for the first time that week. We are camera blocking (running through camera positions) from early in the morning and working to make the transition from rehearsal room to studio floor the smoothest possible, so it's all hands on deck.

We film the couples' run-throughs so we can watch them back and provide feedback. We don't like to change anything at that stage, but it gives us a chance to flag if anything isn't working because we still have 24 hours to fix it. The Executive Producer Sarah and I are like a tag team, running between the studio floor and the gallery all day – I certainly get my steps in!

We wrap at 7.30pm, when the studio is freed up for the band.

Saturday

If there's any element of the costume we guess might be an extra challenge for the celebrity, like a big skirt or a cape, we get it to the couples on Friday, but generally, Saturday is the first time the costume and live music come into the mix.

I'm in the car between 6am and 7am, to make an early start. The couples have two runs in the morning, dancing to the live band for the first time, so Ian and Dave Arch make any necessary tweaks. Then there's the costume run and, after that, a meeting to discuss anything that wardrobe need to change – for instance, if an outfit needs more rhinestones. Between that costume run and the main show, Vicky Gill works miracles!

Knowing we are going live that evening, we're trying to beat the clock to get everything right, getting costumes finished or a prop repainted, so it is exciting. I won't leave the studio until midnight, but the day goes so quickly, especially once the show starts. At that point there's very little we can do, but that's the excitement of the live show and it's a great feeling when it all comes together on the night.

Angela Rippon

As the presenter of the original *Come Dancing* series, Angela Rippon had a ringside seat for the biggest competitions in the dance world. Now it's her turn to take to the dance floor, and she is determined to have a ball.

'I've been a fan of *Strictly* since day one, so I'm looking forward to this adventure,' she says. 'All the people that I know that have done *Strictly* before me have sent emails and messages, and they all said, "You're going to have such fun, however long it lasts, so just enjoy it." So at the end of the day, I decided I'm just going to have fun.'

Born in Plymouth, Angela forged a journalistic career that has now spanned 60 years and led to her fronting a wide variety of TV shows, from hard news and current affairs to quiz shows. As well as being the first female journalist to become a regular newsreader on the BBC, in 1975, she has fronted programmes including *Top Gear*, *Antiques Roadshow*, *Crufts*, *How to Stay Young* and *The Truth About Dementia*, to name but a few. She hosted the original *Come Dancing* between 1988 and 1991 and famously emerged from her news desk, high-kicking her way through a dance routine, on Morecambe and Wise's 1976 Christmas show.

As an ambassador for the Royal Academy of Dance's Silver Swan programme, which aims to get older people back into dance, Angela wants to prove there's no age limit to strutting your stuff.

'I've been involved in dance for a lot of my career,' she says. 'I'm not a dancer but have been associated with it in one way or another. When I made *How to Stay Young* they did proper scientific research that found that dance was the best exercise for 50- to 60-year-olds – it's perfect for all-round mind and body exercise to keep you strong and supple. It's good for balance, stimulates your brain and social activity – it's a package.

'I love dance and I've been promoting dance as a way of keeping strong, fit, agile and balanced, so I suppose I wanted to do the show because of that, and to prove that dance can help you, in so many ways, no matter what your age.'

Angela admits to a few early nerves after signing up for *Strictly* but says meeting partner Kai Widdrington reassured her that she is in safe hands.

'I was a bit apprehensive, but I felt much better after meeting Kai,' she says. 'At that moment you think, "Okay, I can trust this person." I'm so happy to be paired with him. Also, getting to train with all the other celebrities for the group dance was great, and every time we do anything together, it becomes more fun.'

Angela is hoping to stay in long enough to do her favourite dance, the Argentine Tango, but also to celebrate her seventy-ninth birthday on 12 October.

'I look at the skill and the youth and the quality of the other performers and I just keep saying to everybody, "Don't have expectations about what I'm going to achieve,"' she says. 'My mantra is that I can do it, for as long as I can do it. If I can get past my seventy-ninth that would be jolly nice, but every week will be a bonus for me.'

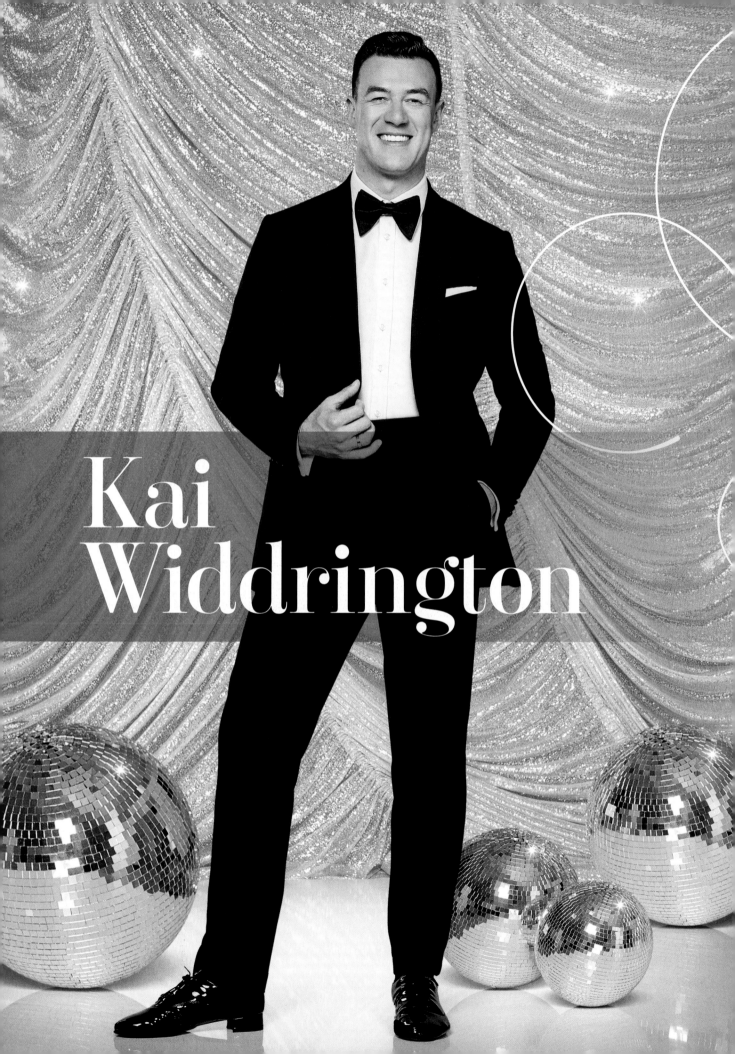

Kai Widdrington

Meeting celebrity partner Angela Rippon in Blackpool's Tower Ballroom was an extra-special moment for Kai and he's hoping fate will lead them back to dance at the iconic venue in November.

'It was lovely to meet Angela in the Tower Ballroom,' he says. 'The story arc is all there because she presented *Come Dancing*, over 30 years ago, and I used to compete there as a young boy. To meet there for the first time was magical.

'I've never danced at Blackpool with my celebrity partner, but the third time's a charm. If we get as far as Blackpool week that would be really special.'

Angela's many years in *Come Dancing* means she is familiar with the ballroom and Latin styles, but Kai says translating that onto the dance floor is another matter.

'Knowing a lot about something and doing it are two different things,' he says. 'We're at square one and in the same boat as everyone else. But Angela is a dream student. I couldn't ask for a better person to be teaching. There's definitely some potential there.'

Born in Southampton, Kai became World Junior Latin-American Champion at the age of 14, in 2010. Two years later, he was a finalist on *Britain's Got Talent* and he returned in 2018 with a dance group, alongside Neil and Katya. He was a finalist twice on Ireland's *Dancing with the Stars* before joining the UK show as a professional dancer in 2021. Last year, he was partnered with *Loose Women* star Kaye Adams but was first to leave the competition.

'Kaye was absolutely brilliant to teach,' he says. 'We got on like a house on fire. She's been checking in this series, saying, "I hope Angela's doing great." She's a really lovely woman and I'm glad I got to spend those few weeks with her, teaching her.'

Kai also made a friend for life in last year's winner, Hamza Yassin.

'If there ever was a worthy champion, it's Hamza,' he says. 'He was just fabulous. He is one of the nicest people I've ever met in my entire life. It's a pleasure to call him a friend.'

As well as making it to the Tower Ballroom, Kai is keen to perform Angela's favourite dance during the series.

'I'm looking forward to the themed weeks, especially Movie Week and Halloween,' he says. 'I'd also love to get Angela to do an Argentine Tango, because she's very excited about that. Most of all I would love to get Angela to Blackpool, so I'm manifesting that.

'But, as I said the moment I met her, my number-one priority is that she enjoys this experience, because the celebrity only gets to do it once and I want her to have a laugh. My main goal is for her to look back with nothing but positive memories and say, "I'm really glad I did *Strictly*."'

Nikita Kanda

Radio presenter Nikita is swapping the turntables for the Tango and can't wait to show the world what she can do.

'I can't believe I was asked to do it,' she says. 'It was a "pinch me" moment. It's such an iconic show, I literally could not say no. It is a dream to do this show.

'It's so different to radio and I'm used to being behind the mic. On screen, I've reported for *The One Show* and other TV shows, but I don't think there's another show like *Strictly*, so this is going to be a whole different ballgame. It's always nerve-wracking to put yourself out there, and obviously *Strictly* is one of the biggest shows on TV, but I'm excited because people get to see a different side of me, not just as a radio presenter.'

Birmingham-born Nikita studied film and screen media at university before launching her career on Zee TV. She began presenting a Saturday-afternoon show on BBC Asian Network in March 2021 and is now hosting the station's *Breakfast* show, interviewing guests from Sandra Oh to Nick Jonas.

Nikita, who is paired with series-20 finalist Gorka Márquez, says she has no dance experience other than club nights. 'I've done acting and a bit of singing in the past, but never dancing. I was in Ibiza recently and my signature move was literally just putting my hand up in the air and going from side to side with my arm waving.'

The radio star has been getting some encouragement from fellow presenter Anita Rani, who danced in series 13.

'Anita Rani messaged me and she said, "Have fun, throw yourself into it. You're going to be great so just enjoy it,"' she says. 'I'm yet to have a coffee with her, so I haven't had my full-on debrief with her, but I'm sure we will.'

With no formal dress code for her radio work, Nikita is looking forward to putting on the glitz for *Strictly* and adores the outfits she's been fitted for so far.

'That's the best bit,' she says. 'I want to take them home. I want to sleep in them! The costume team is just phenomenal, so every single outfit is amazing. I love getting glam. I am all about the make-up and hair – throw as much glitter on me as you want!'

Nikita's favourite *Strictly* moment of the past was Judi Love's twerking routine to Sean Paul's 'Get Busy', which she calls 'epic', and Rose Ayling-Ellis's iconic Couple's Choice dance, which 'gave me goosebumps and made me cry'.

Now she's hoping to create some unforgettable moments of her own and says she is not thinking which celebrities might be her toughest competition.

'I want positive vibes because I just think everyone's so different,' she says.

With her eye firmly on the prize, however, Nikita says her mum is already clearing a space on the mantelpiece.

'I am eyeing that trophy, definitely,' she says. 'Obviously it'd be a dream come true to win it. My mum said "You better bring that back, I need it on my fireplace!" Whatever I do, I give 100 per cent, so obviously you want to aim for getting to the Final. If I could, it would be a dream. But either way, it's still amazing taking part in the show.'

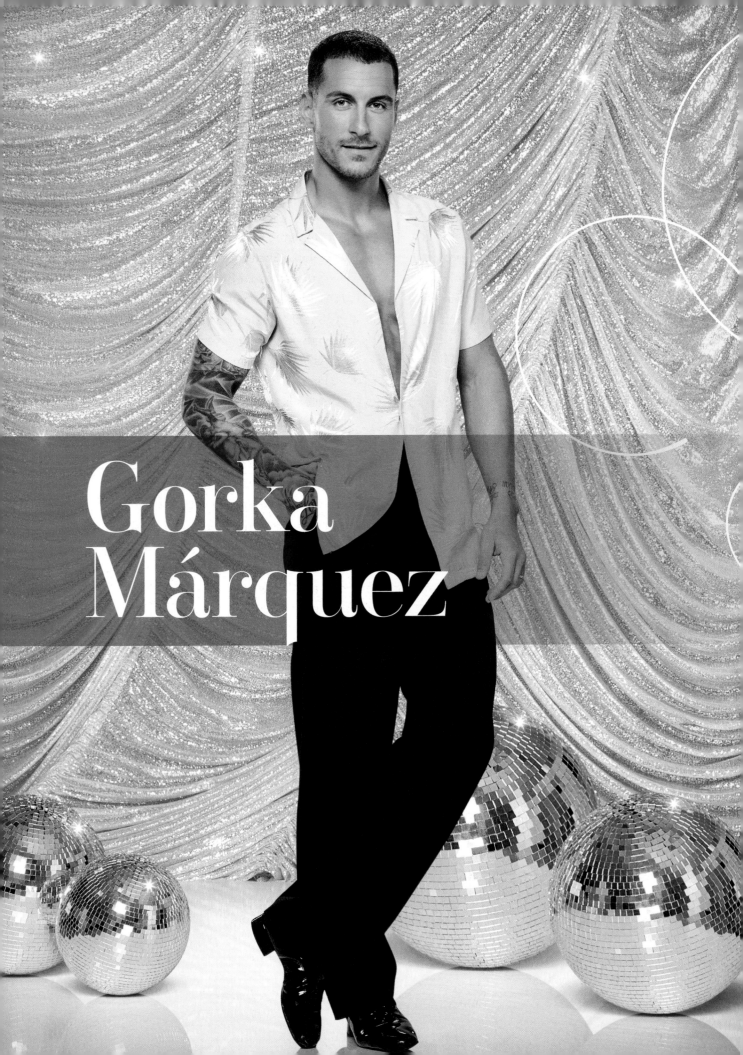

Gorka Márquez

A three-time finalist, with Alexandra Burke, Maisie Smith and last year's partner Helen Skelton, Gorka is paired with broadcaster Nikita Kanda for his eighth series as a *Strictly* pro.

'Nikita is lots of fun, positive and enthusiastic,' he says. 'She has a fresh energy and we laugh a lot. We have a similar sense of humour and we clicked instantly, which makes the process more fun. Also, we both love a chat! I feel like I know her well already. We're both very excited.'

Nikita is starting from scratch and Gorka sees that as a plus.

'I love someone who's never danced before,' he says. 'Her job has nothing to do with performing in terms of singing, acting or musical theatre, which is good because she's very raw. She is committed, so she's putting in the hours and the effort. She listens to me and that's essential. I think she has potential, and the most important thing is that she always smiles when she's dancing and puts joy into it. Even if she's struggling with a dance, she'll have a beaming smile and is always giggling.'

While it's early days, Gorka thinks his new pupil may gravitate towards the party dances. 'Nikita is sassy and cheeky, with plenty of fire, and she loves Shakira, so I think she will like Latin dances more,' he says. 'She might find ballroom dances more difficult.'

Although Nikita is still hosting the BBC Asian Network *Breakfast Show*, they are training for six or seven hours a day and Gorka says progress is about quality, not quantity. 'You could do 12 hours a day but would probably spend two hours having breaks. The important thing is to be fully committed in the hours we have. Sometimes two hours can be more productive than seven.'

Gorka was born in Bilbao, Spain, and took up dance at 11, representing his country in the World Latin Championships in 2010 and the semi-finals of the 2012 World DanceSport Federation World Cup. He joined *Strictly* in 2016 and last year he completed his Grand Final hat-trick with presenter Helen Skelton, bagging a perfect score for their *Cabaret*-inspired Couple's Choice.

'With Helen, what you see is what you get,' he says. 'She's the same person on and off the screen, a normal, down-to-earth human. Sometimes in life you meet special people that leave a stamp on your life and stay in your life forever. Helen is one of those.'

Gorka says Helen's confidence grew throughout the show and he has fond memories of the dance that proved a turning point for her.

'The "Mein Herr" routine was our number one and Helen stole the hearts of the nation,' he says. 'But I also love the Quickstep in Blackpool because that was when she started believing in herself and feeling confident. She was up North, her family and kids were there, and it was a special weekend.'

'Getting into the Final was amazing. It was a celebration of our journey and the last time that we were going to dance together, so I said, "Let's enjoy this one more time."'

With Nikita, Gorka is making sure she has fun every day.

'I can't control how long my partner is on the show,' he says. 'I do my best to teach them a routine every week, and I want them to leave the show having had the best time. You only get one chance, so I want them to come in with an open mind, ready for anything, to let themselves go, get lost in the experience and enjoy it to the fullest. Then, when you walk away, whichever week it is, you know you gave it everything and had a fabulous time.'

Tribute to Len

Earlier this year, the *Strictly* family lost a much-loved member when original head judge Len Goodman passed away.

From the opening show, Len's quick wit, sparkling personality and unsurpassed knowledge of ballroom and Latin dance helped make *Strictly Come Dancing* the global success it is today. The news of his passing, in April, caused an outpouring of love and messages from around the globe.

Executive Producer Sarah James says: 'Len was more than the head judge on *Strictly*, he was a beloved colleague and friend who meant so much to so many. He was supportive, honest and kind to all the couples who he judged on the *Strictly* dance floor and made everyone feel special. A true gentleman and a people person, he could always be relied on to lift the mood with his quick wit or a "Len-ism". His warmth and humour were not just reserved for on screen, and the whole *Strictly* team are deeply saddened to hear of his passing. Above all, he was a family man, and our thoughts are with his loved ones.'

Born in Kent, Len worked as a barrow boy and apprentice welder in London and took

up dancing as a teenager after a foot injury stopped him playing football. He went on to compete in major competitions with partner Cherry Kingston, before opening his own dance school in Dartford, Kent, and becoming a well-known judge on the competitive circuit. Before being asked to join the *Strictly* panel, Len coached many a professional dancer, including our very own judges Shirley Ballas and Anton Du Beke.

'Len was a legend in the dance industry before he was known to TV viewers, and everybody in the industry has grown up with him,' says Shirley. 'I knew Len for 40 years. He was a teacher of mine, a colleague and an adjudicator throughout my dancing career. My former dance partner, Corky, and I trained with him. He used to say, "Take your work seriously, but don't take yourself too seriously." He was iconic in every way.'

When *Strictly Come Dancing* was first conceived in 2004, Len's name was put forward as a possible judge and he auditioned on his sixtieth birthday. He was an instant hit with viewers, getting a laugh in his first show with a phrase borrowed from his grandad, when he described one routine as 'all sausage and no sizzle'.Other memorable comments included 'You floated across that floor like butter on a crumpet' and 'You're just like a trifle – fruity at the top, but a little bit spongy down below', as well as his catchphrase 'pickle my walnuts' and his unique way of saying, 'Se-VEN!'

'Len never failed to light up the screen,' says Tess. 'He liked a laugh and he didn't take this showbusiness lark, which came late in life, too seriously. After years of work in the competitive world of dance, he found himself working on a primetime television show and catapulted into the limelight, but he took to sitting on that

judging panel, with an audience of 10 million or more, like a duck to water. He was warm and genuine, and the nation took him to their hearts.

'*Strictly* is a show born from the ballroom dancing scene,' Tess explains, 'so what greater authority could we have sitting on the panel than Len Goodman, the don of ballroom dancing? Many of our pro dancers had been in competitions where he had judged, and they had huge respect for him. His love of dance and his knowledge was all-encompassing, so viewers knew they were in safe hands.'

As well as heading the UK panel until 2016, Len judged the US version of the show *Dancing with the Stars,* alongside Bruno Tonioli, until 2022, and there were many weeks when the shows overlapped, meaning they had to jet between the two countries.

'We would spend three days in London and three days in LA and we could not have done it without each other,' says Bruno. 'We had a complete trust and watched each other's back. We were like brothers in arms.'

Len, who leaves behind his wife Sue, son James and two grandchildren, was the King of Ballroom and a household name on both sides of the Atlantic. His legacy lives on, through the many people he inspired, and he will be sadly missed by all.

Tributes

TESS DALY

'Len was the most charismatic man I ever had the pleasure to meet. I'll never forget that twinkling eye, cheeky grin and wicked sense of humour. He was full of fun, and it felt like a gift to be in his presence and receive the Len sparkly smile. Obviously, he was a genuine authority in dance, but also a brilliant raconteur and showman. He was a total gentleman and an all-round lovely bloke, and his warmth and authenticity shone through the screen. He was loved by all and is deeply missed.'

CLAUDIA WINKLEMAN

'Len was pure magic. I loved working with him. When we did Len's Masterclass on *It Takes Two*, we would end up crying with laughter. In my family, we don't say "seven" like we used to – he taught us a whole new way of saying that number. Len was charm itself, funny and clever, but also the most humble person I've ever met in television. If we offered him a cup of tea, he'd insist on making it himself and he never wanted anyone to make a fuss. But what Len didn't know about dance is not worth knowing and he taught me so much. If he liked a dance, it meant everything to the celebrity and the professional, because they all wanted to impress him. He was an amazing human being and is a very sad loss.'

SHIRLEY BALLAS

'Len played a huge role in *Strictly*'s success, because it is still, to this day, based around ballroom and Latin, and, because he was so well qualified, he was able to critique in a way that nobody else could. He was so sincere, so loyal, so honest, and people could use his words as a learning tool. He was funny and quick-witted, but he also gave great advice to the couples and helped them improve from week to week. He never told couples they were bad; it was about telling them how to get better.

'When Len stood down from *Strictly* and I got the job, people asked what it was like to fill his shoes. But there was no way anybody could fill Len's iconic shoes, so I stuck my fluffy slippers inside them and did my best. He was a wonderful man and will be deeply missed.'

CRAIG REVEL HORWOOD

'I didn't know Len before *Strictly*, but I instantly got along with him. He was a cheeky chappy, very funny, and his comments made me laugh all the time. We fought like cat and dog, of course, on set, but that never travelled backstage. There was a wonderful dynamic between us, which I miss. We got on like a house on fire and I enjoyed going out for dinner with Len and his wife, Sue. I shared a dressing room and transport with him on the Live Tour for many, many years, so we were close.'Len's style of judging was his own and no one could replicate it. He even made the numeral "se-VEN" so famous, as well as "a 10 from Len". He was a great comic, making everyone laugh on set and off, and he had a one-liner for absolutely everything. He's going to be sadly missed.'

ANTON DU BEKE

'Len, my dear friend of nearly 45 years, was a wonderful character and universally loved. Funny, entertaining, thoughtful, clever and fascinating – I was very lucky to know him.

'As a dancer, you wanted him to like what you did. His opinion was everything. That, for me, remained throughout my entire career – whether as a young lad when he was my dance judge or in the *Strictly* ballroom. *Strictly* would not be *Strictly* without Len's exceptional impact, and naturally I spoke to him when I joined the judging panel. His simple advice to me was, "Say what you see and be yourself." That's exactly how Len was and how I'll always remember him.'

BRUNO TONIOLI

'Working with Len on both the UK and US shows, we trusted each other completely. We knew each other so well and I had total confidence that whatever ball I threw in the air, he would come back with a winner. It was like playing a game with Roger Federer. I always say, "You're only as good as the people you work with," and working with Len and the original judging panel set a template. It was incredible working with someone who is always up for it and absolutely fearless. He was an original. There are people that you can never replicate, and he was a one-off. You could never find another Len.'

Ellie Leach

Known to the nation as *Coronation Street*'s ill-fated Faye Windass, for the last 12 years Ellie has had little to smile about on camera – but signing up for *Strictly* has her grinning from ear to ear.

'I've played a character all my life and I'm excited to let people see my own personality and see the real me, not the character I played in *Corrie*,' she says. 'I've always wanted to do *Strictly*. Ever since I was younger, I've been obsessed with dancing and watching dancing, and I used to do tap and ballet when I was younger, but I'm not trained. I think coming out of *Coronation Street*, it's amazing to have a new experience and do something that I have never done before.'

Coming from a whole family of *Strictly* fans, Ellie says her mum is over the moon that she's taking to the hallowed dance floor – and getting the *Strictly* makeover.

'I'm so excited, and my family are buzzing for me,' she says. 'My mum is saying, "I can't wait for you to wear all the dresses and get glammed up." I can't wait either. Give me the tan, give me the sequins, give me the make-up, the hair, the glitter – everything. When I'm trying on outfits in the costume department I ask, "Do I have to take it off?" I want to keep it on forever.'

Manchester-born Ellie started acting at an early age, appearing in adverts, the independent movie *A Boy Called Dad* and drama *Moving On* before landing the role of Faye at the age of 10. Her time on the cobbles has seen her nominated for several awards for hard-hitting storylines. She left the soap earlier this year.

Ellie, who jokes that her signature dance move is the worm, is thrilled to be partnered with series-20 finalist Vito Coppola and thinks one of the biggest challenges ahead will be performing live.

'I've never done live TV before,' she says. 'Obviously, when I did *Coronation Street* it's pre-recorded and I think the live situation is a bit scary, but I'm excited. Again, it's something different, so I'm excited to experience that.'

Ellie has had plenty of support from former co-stars, and series-20 contestant Kym Marsh has urged her to enjoy every minute.

'Kym didn't give me any dancing advice but just said, "It's amazing, the best time ever. You'll have so much fun but cherish the moments, because it goes so fast."'

While she is fulfilling a lifetime ambition to learn Latin and ballroom, Ellie is also angling for a place in the Final.

'You'd be silly not to have your eye on the Glitterball trophy,' she says. 'For me, winning is great, but it's always the taking part that counts. I'm just really excited to have fun, but obviously to win would be amazing, an absolute dream come true, but also, being part of this journey is already a dream come true. I'm really excited to ride the wave and see where I end up.'

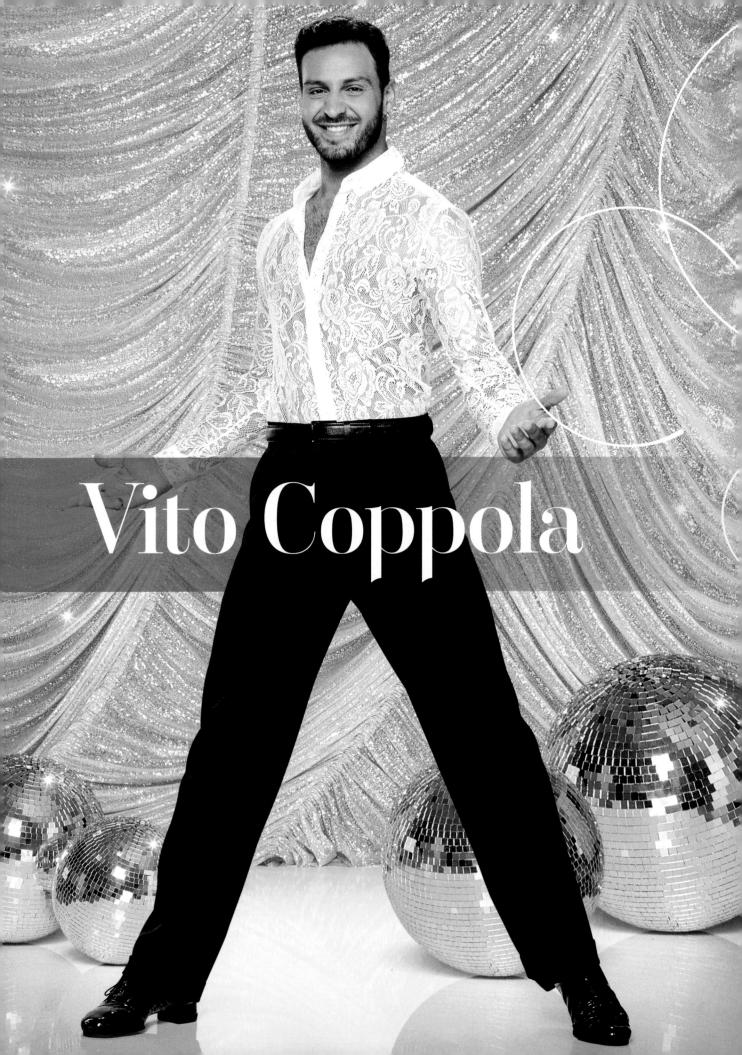

Vito Coppola

In his debut year, Italian professional dancer Vito powered through to the Final with singer Fleur East. For this series, he is thrilled to be paired with *Coronation Street* star Ellie Leach and says his new partner is showing promise.

'As soon as I met Ellie I couldn't wait to get in the studio,' he says. 'She's lovely, so sweet, but at the same time she's very determined. She wants to learn and is very conscious of the things she wants to improve, before even learning the steps, and asked me to work on her posture and frame. We are already motivating each other. I'm very happy.'

Vito says a funny exchange during the launch-show rehearsals showed that Ellie has untapped potential that even she doesn't appreciate.

'There's a move where we're waving with our arms, and she said, "Vito, I can't do this movement." While she was showing me which movement it was, she did it perfectly. She's not even conscious of her own capability. She's very well coordinated. We need to work on her posture and technique, but I can see that it's there.'

While Ellie might be more suited to Latin than ballroom, Vito thinks that could all change with training.

'She likes the Latin because she feels more free and doesn't have so many restrictions,' he says. 'But from the experience I had with Fleur, I know that whatever you think at the beginning, your partner can surprise you. Samba might be Ellie's best dance, but she could dance a Waltz or a Tango, which are a totally different frame and posture, that nobody expects. Everything depends on muscle memory and how her body absorbs the information. Everyone is different.'

As an actor, Ellie can bring character to the dance – and Vito is hoping to learn from his pupil.

'We used to study acting because, in the dance, you have to be in the part and the mood,' he says. 'The fact that she's an actor makes my life easier, but it's also an opportunity for us to have an exchange of knowledge. I can learn from her acting skills as she learns from me how to dance.'

Hailing from the Italian region of Salerno, Vito comes from a dancing family. He won his Italian championship at nine and two years later was called to join the Italian team in the international championships in Germany, going on to become world champion and European champion. In 2021, Vito won Italy's *Ballando con le Stelle* (*Dancing with the Stars*) with singer Arisa, and a year later he became a finalist on *Strictly* with Fleur.

'Last year was such a memorable year and I'm so grateful,' he says. 'It was like being caught up in a beautiful tornado. I was so lucky to have Fleur for my first *Strictly* journey, and I found a friend and sister for life. Every rehearsal was unique and we had so much fun.

'Getting to the Final was an emotional moment and we couldn't believe it was real. The fact we had been in a few dance-offs made it even more challenging and interesting – an emotional roller-coaster. But this is *Strictly* and it's about the journey, not just about getting to the Final.'

While their Couple's Choice, to a Destiny's Child megamix, blew the judges away and landed the first 40 of the series, Vito has two more dances that stick in his mind.

'Every week, we tried to make it special,' he says. 'But I loved the Argentine Tango, because it was the week after our first dance-off, which was the toughest week, and we scored two 10s and two 9s. The showdance was special because we wanted to tell people our *Strictly* story, and while we were dancing we both had tears in our eyes. That was one of the best feelings, because we were really living the moment and the emotion was real.'

Crossword

A *Strictly* teatime teaser to get the grey cells tingling.

Across

1. & 6 down, former *Strictly* pro who presents *It Takes Two* (7, 7)

3. Surname of the pro who danced with Kym Marsh in series 20 (2, 5)

8. Former winner McFadden or finalist Sugg (3)

10. Ms Rice, series-17 contestant who loves a challenge (6)

11. Dave Arch leads this and provides the music for the routines (4)

13. First name of *Loose Women* star and comedian who partnered 3 across in series 19 (4)

14. First name of series-14 winner Oduba (3)

15. Blue star Lee, who partnered Nadiya Bychkova in series 16 (4)

16. Stage show or film with songs, celebrated in a *Strictly* special themed week (7)

17. Comedian Conley, who danced in series 15 (5)

18. First name of Scottish comedian and series-15 contestant Calman (5)

19. Surname of 'Mysterious Girl' singer who made it to week 10 with 1 across (5)

22. Singer of 'Shout' who appeared in series 9 (4)

25. Welsh professional Ms Dowden (3)

26. Ms Bunton and Ms Barton (4)

27. First name of Olympic gold-medallist swimmer who partnered 21 down in series 19 (4)

28. Surname of series-20 comedian contestant who partnered Johannes Radebe (6)

30. Former champion and star of The Wanted, Mr McGuiness (3)

31. Saturdays singer and former finalist Ms Bridge (7)

32. Actress May Foote, who partnered Giovanni Pernice to the series-13 Grand Final (7)

Down

2. Argentine or Ballroom (5)

4. Country of origin for Giovanni, Graziano and Vito (5)

5. Full name of TV judge and former *Strictly* contestant (6, 6)

6. See 1 across

7. First name of 'Mysterious Girl' singer who made it to week 10 with 1 across (5)

9. Surname of presenter AJ, who partnered Kai Widdrington in series 19 (5)

12. Ukrainian pro whose partners include Ellie Simmonds and Tilly Ramsay (6, 6)

20. The dance of love (5)

21. Ms Jones, pro partner of 27 across (5)

23. '_____ the Sea', the song from *The Little Mermaid*, which saw Scott Mills famously dress as a crab for an iconic routine (5)

24. First name of *Strictly* judge Ms Mabuse (5)

29. The paddle most dreaded by the celebrities, which has only been shown 11 times in the history of the show (3)

Strictly Sustainable

Strictly is the epitome of glitz and glamour, but that doesn't mean it costs the earth. From using biodegradable glitter to recycling the fabulous dresses, each team on the show has been working hard in recent years to reduce the environmental impact of the series.

'At *Strictly*, we have made significant progress in reducing our carbon footprint and continue to work with our suppliers and crew to find new ways to improve sustainability across the show,' says Production Executive Kate Jones. Liquid glitter is used to give the dancers that extra sparkle, and since 2018 almost all of it has been sourced from specialist environmentally friendly suppliers whose products are biodegradable. There has also been a significant reduction in the use of microplastics, and only biodegradable make-up wipes are used by the team. The special effects for each routine

– from pyrotechnics to confetti – are created using a minimum of 95 per cent biodegradable products, while props for group numbers are upcycled for use elsewhere. Single-use plastic has seen a significant reduction and bottled water has been eliminated from the production, with reusable bottles being introduced for all the crew, production team and talent. Audience members are still able to buy water on site, but it is only available in more eco-friendly cartons. In backstage catering, where the cast and crew refuel, all cutlery and packaging are now compostable.

The camera crew relies on call sheets, which used to be printed but are now accessed using iPads, helping to reduce printing by 80 per cent. Many meetings are now scheduled via video link to cut down on unnecessary travel, and documents are shared digitally. Over 70 per cent of the lighting is energy efficient and the generators used in the studio run on hydrotreated vegetable oil (HVO), a renewable biofuel, which reduces carbon emissions by up to 90 per cent.

When it comes to the fabulous outfits, around 50 per cent are reused, with group-number and previous-series costumes being upcycled, thanks to the creativity of Head of Wardrobe Vicky Gill and her amazing team. Those that can't be recycled for the show also go to good homes.

'Everything gets used at some point – nothing's a throw-away,' says Vicky. 'Some garments move on afterwards, to be hired and reused around the world within the *Dancing with the Stars* family; others will go to a dancewear company to be used within the competitive ballroom and Latin world, and others are donated to theatre schools or amateur groups. We're helping the planet by remaking and reusing, but storage also has an environmental impact, so it is better to give away some garments than to expand storage.'

Those companies who support the production, such as hotels and catering companies, provide a green memo, which details how they minimise their own impact on the planet, and all taxis used for the show are eco-friendly cars.

'Each production is required to complete the Albert Carbon Calculator tool, which was set up to encourage film and TV productions to reduce their environmental impact, and this helps us recognise which areas need improving,' says Kate. 'Each year we continue to look at ways to improve the sustainability of the production, the biggest challenge being the scale and length of the production. We work closely with the BBC sustainability team to explore new ways of working and attend monthly meetings where ideas are shared between productions.'

Craig loves getting his dancing shoes on whenever he can in the series, and this year he particularly enjoyed the launch-show routine with his fellow judges. But he was also busy casting his eye over the latest *Strictly* stars.

'The launch show was absolutely fantastic and we all had a brilliant time. It's always a great way to start the series with a bang,' he says. 'Plus we get to see all the celebrities lining up and dancing for the first time and they really are a fabulous group of people this year. The line-up is brilliant, a real cross-section of the celebrity community, and the pairings are inspired. I can't wait for the competition to start. It's going to be an incredible year.'

The huge range of the *Strictly* stars, aged between 20 and 78, is a reflection of the universal appeal of ballroom and Latin, says Craig.

'It is what we're always saying, that dance is for young and old,' he says. 'Dances don't have to be too strenuous, but it's a great way for everyone to keep the joints in check, and to get the blood circulating. Music, as we know, also helps people mentally and dancing is fun because you are doing it with someone else. You don't necessarily think you're exercising if you're doing a little Waltz, but you are and that's what's great about it.'

Australian-born Craig, who danced in West End shows before becoming a director and choreographer, looks back fondly on last year's Grand Final and says any one of the four celebrities who made it through could have won.

'It was absolutely extraordinary,' he says. 'I loved every single person in that Final. Molly Rainford, Fleur East and Helen Skelton were all great, as well as Hamza. The nation loved him and winning *Strictly* changed his life. He was in floods of tears at the Final.'

As director of the *Strictly Come Dancing Live Tour*, Craig got to spend more time with the series-20 couples as they toured their routines to fans around the country. Highlights included Fleur's Destiny's Child tribute, Hamza's strongman Salsa, Molly's Quickstep and Helen's *Cabaret*-inspired Couple's Choice.

'We had such a great time. The tour is a lot more relaxed, and it's amazing to be able to bring those spellbinding dances to a live audience of *Strictly*'s wonderful fans.'

Looking ahead, Craig is itching to see what the latest recruits can achieve on the dance floor.

'I am looking forward to getting back into the competition again, because that's what I really love,' he says. 'I'm excited to be going to Blackpool again and, of course, all the celebrities want to get to Blackpool. And I can't wait to see all the group dances, which are always *fab-u-lous!*'

Craig Revel Horwood

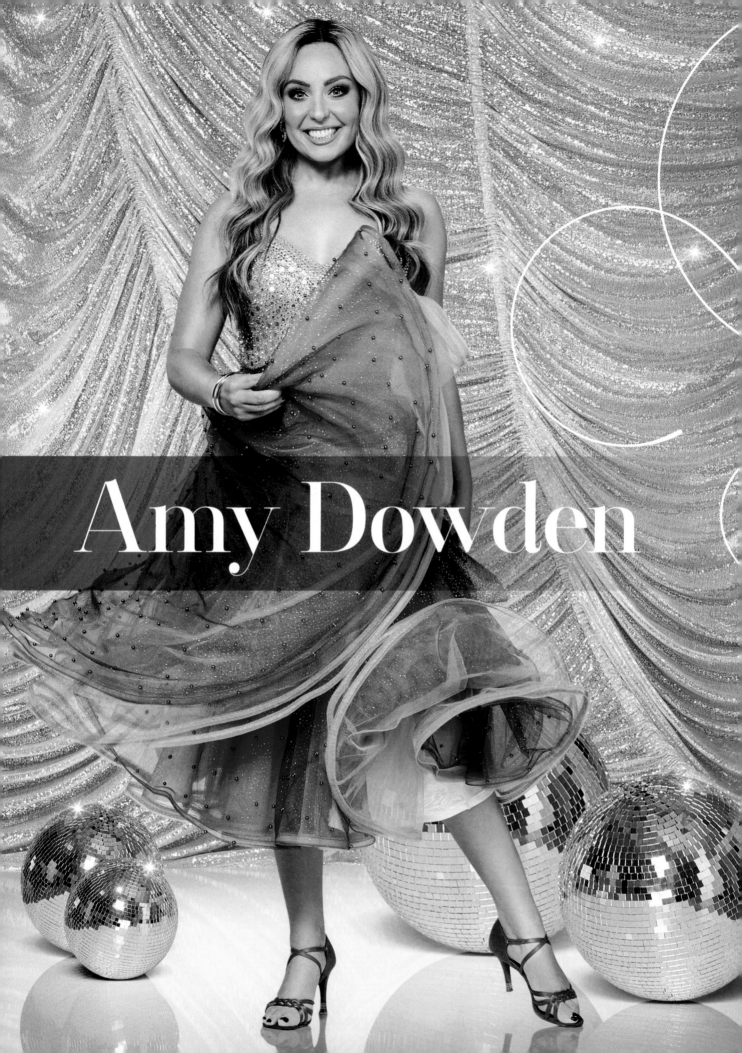

Amy Dowden

Welsh professional dancer Amy has partnered six celebrities since joining the *Strictly* team and made it to the Grand Final with Karim Zeroual in series 17. But she says this year the finalists are hard to predict.

'The cast is absolutely brilliant,' she says. 'Sometimes when you watch the first group dance you think, "They're going to be in the Final," but this series it's really open.

'There are definitely some movers in there, but until you've been in the training room and had that one-on-one tuition with your partner, it's difficult to gauge. Being in that training room and working with your professional is totally different to the first group number. I'm excited to see who progresses throughout and falls in love with dancing.'

Amy, who was unable to perform at the start of the series due to chemotherapy treatment, was moved by the professionals' group dance in the launch show, which was dedicated to her.

'Watching the pros was emotional to begin with, because obviously I want to be there dancing with them, but they did that lovely performance for me and when Tess and Claudia sent me a message, it was so touching,' she says. 'I just loved watching all the pairings and seeing them chatting in the Clauditorium, Claud's area, so I was laughing and excited for them all. The pros are my friends, my *Strictly* family, so it was just what I needed.'

Amy also loved seeingall four judges showing off their own particular dance skills. 'I was totally wowed by the judges' dancing,' she says. 'I loved how their personalities come out. It had drama and excitement. It clearly shows why they are in their chairs, judging week in, week out. It reminds the audience of their qualities, how lucky we are to have them, and also shows the passion that they still have for dancing.'

Born and raised in Caerphilly, Amy took up dancing at eight and is a four-time British National Finalist and a British National Champion. She joined *Strictly* in 2017 and last year she made it to Halloween Week with *EastEnders* star James Bye.

'James was absolutely brilliant and I was so proud of him,' she says. 'We had such a great time and he was definitely a ballroom boy. James had a busy filming schedule on *EastEnders* and a young family, but I was in awe of how he managed to fit it all in. He worked really hard and fell in love with dancing and the show. He's become a really good friend.'

Ahead of this series, the former finalist has some sound advice for the new recruits and says trust is the key to *Strictly* success.

'It's not about how fast you can learn the moves; it's about embracing the show and enjoying the process, trusting your partner and going along with the ride,' she says. 'If you fall in love with the dancing, the nation sees that. It's about not getting wrapped up in the scores or the comments but trusting in what your partner and the judges are telling you.

'You never know when that journey might be over, so make the most of every moment of magic and fabulousness. If the audience see how much you love it, they will be captivated and get lost in your performance. If you've done that, you can win.'

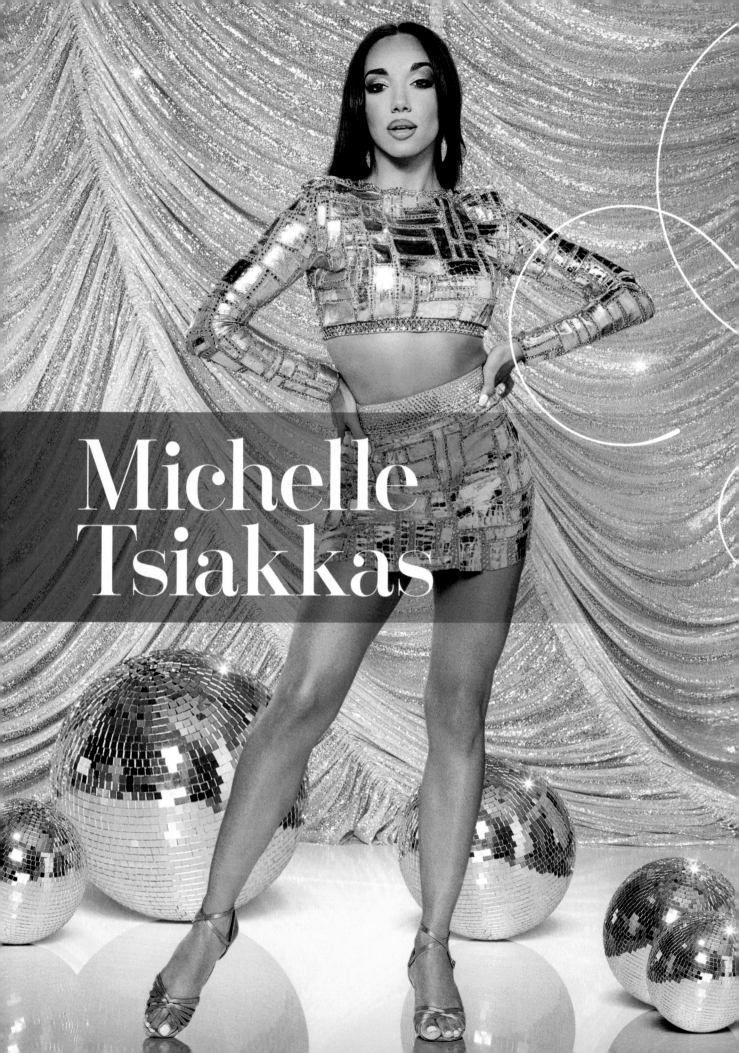

Michelle
Tsiakkas

Going into her second year as part of the *Strictly* professional dancer team, Michelle is excited to be returning and to be reunited with her fellow pros.

'Dancing on *Strictly* and continuing to work with the team is really a dream,' she says. 'I am looking forward to being in the group dances and the special weeks, like Blackpool, which is an amazing place to dance. It's great to be back in the fold with my fellow pros after a few months of not seeing each other, because they are a really lovely bunch. It's like one big family.'

Born and raised in Cyprus, Michelle began competing from six and was Cypriot national champion for 10 consecutive years. She studied architecture at the University of Kent, in Canterbury, before returning to dance full time at 19. Being new to the world of TV, Michelle's debut year in *Strictly* proved an eye-opener.

'It was all very new to me and a lot of things were quite overwhelming at the start, but I quickly got used to how everything works in TV,' she says. 'Everyone was so welcoming, and if I had any questions, they were really accommodating. I think that's why it's such a great team, because everyone is so friendly, passionate about what they do and good at what they do. It's a great environment to learn from people around you and to prosper in what you love to do.'

A *Strictly* fan since she was a child, Michelle says it was a dream to work on the show.

'I was stunned at how fast-paced it is, because what we see on TV is the final result, but putting things together, it's go, go, go, from morning until midnight, continuously changing hair and make-up looks and outfits between dances,' she says. 'Because all the teams are so impressive, the live shows happen seamlessly, and everything is so well planned and organised. There are a lot of things to take into consideration that you don't think about as a viewer, but all the different departments work together so well to put on a great show.

'The thing that surprised me most is how quickly Vicky Gill and the costume team put the outfits together. It never crossed my mind before but they have so much to do and they can whip something amazing together in a few minutes, taking bits of materials here and there, adding a fringe and stones. That really impressed me.'

Earlier this year, Michelle also joined the touring company for *Strictly Live!* and had a blast meeting fans and dancing in arenas across the country.

'It was so much fun. I love the feeling of performing for crowds of up to 10,000 people,' she says. 'I don't think there are any words to describe what an amazing feeling that was. A dream come true. Right before stepping on stage, on the very first show, I got quite emotional and nearly cried. I couldn't believe it was actually happening. It was very special.'

Michelle has also been touched at how *Strictly* superfans instantly took her to their hearts. 'I didn't expect it because I'm new and the public haven't seen me with a celebrity partner, but I have been getting a lot of love. *Strictly* fans love the show and somehow found this connection with me, and it's really nice that they support me.'

Going into the twenty-first series, presenter Claudia is keen to meet the new *Strictly* stars and see them throw some shapes on the dance floor.

'I can't wait for the first week, when we see them dance,' she says. 'That is my favourite part of the series. As soon as we start rehearsing for the launch show, we all feel really buzzed.

'The group dances are always brilliant and I love watching those every year. But as well as our amazing pros, I have to mention Dave Arch because the work he and his band and the live singers do is phenomenal. I can't wait to get back in the studio and to see those live numbers.

'I love working with Tess, who is the loveliest person in the whole world, as well as everybody behind the scenes. It's the same crew every year so we just fall in with each other. It is like a big reunion and I can't wait.'

Claudia, who has co-hosted the results show since 2010 and main show since 2014, says she is astounded at the names on this year's leader board.

'The *Strictly* producers have done it again, and the line-up is absolutely phenomenal,' she says. 'I cannot wait to meet them. They're all terrific. It is such an honour that Angela Rippon would say "yes" – we almost all cried. Les Dennis is a national treasure, as is Annabel Croft. Every single one of the celebrities is great. I love the fact that it spans all ages. Fingers crossed, it's going to be a bumper year.'

Although Claudia is excited for every minute of the new series, she has some particular highlights each year.

'Obviously the Grand Final makes us all cry and I absolutely love Blackpool week,' she says.

'I also love it when they go to two routines in one week. I don't know how they do it. They're already learning one routine in a week, which is hard, but then going from one to two ramps it up, especially if they've got very different dances. That's always quite tense. I couldn't do it. I'd be absolutely terrible. I can't remember what I had for breakfast, let alone where my foot should go.'

Claudia also reveals she has a favourite dance, which she looks forward to each year. 'I love all of them, but the Argentine Tango is the one I get really excited about and they don't normally bring one out until week four or five. It's the most unbelievable dance. I still remember the first time I saw Tango champs Flavia Cacace and Vincent Simone do it. Our jaws hit the floor. It's like ice skating while holding 700 plates.'

As always, the winning couple from the previous year dance for one last time on the launch show, and Claudia says the return of Hamza Yassin and Jowita Przystał is a boost for the new recruits.

'It's great when we bring back the reigning champion because only they can tell the cast what they need to do to win,' she says. 'We try to advise the celebrities, but Hamza can sit there, look at them all and say, "Guys, this is how I did it." Hamza was just magic.'

Claudia was impressed by the standard of last year's Grand Final and says all four finalists were worthy. 'I loved last year,' she says. 'Every year is my favourite but every year it just gets better. I loved Hamza and all the finalists. Every year, I think, "They can't better that," and then they do.'

Claudia Winkleman

She stunned *Strictly* fans with her incredible routines, bagged the first 40 of series 20 and made it through to the Final with partner Vito Coppola. Now Fleur is celebrating a new *Strictly* role, as co-presenter on *It Takes Two*.

'I'm so excited. I can't wait,' she says. 'It only really sank in when it was announced, and I got a huge reaction from the professional dancers and everybody on the team at *Strictly*, saying, "Fleur, this is incredible." They were so complimentary and genuinely happy for me. Vito jumped up and down; he was so emotional. He was genuinely proud.'

Fleur is fronting *It Takes Two* on Monday and Tuesday, Janette takes the reins on Wednesday and Thursday, and the pair will host alternate Fridays. While they are only together for the first and last show, the co-hosts are already friends, having bonded on the live tour, which Janette presented.

'When I got the *It Takes Two* job, Janette told me, "You understand the process, you know what the celebrities are going through, and you know the pros and the team." She said to be myself and to ask the things I want to know, as a fan of the show.'

Londoner Fleur, who shot to fame in *The X Factor* before scoring a string of hits and becoming a presenter on Hits Radio, is overjoyed to have danced her way to last year's Grand Final.

'I didn't know how far I would go because I was in the dance-off early on, in week three, and there was a lot of competition,' she says. 'So to get to the Grand Final was the most incredible feeling, because when you're in the bubble and enjoying it, you don't want it to end. It didn't really matter who lifted the trophy. I felt I'd won the experience and that was the most important thing.'

The couple's week-four Argentine Tango was a 'stand-out' for Fleur and she loved her Samba, which was 'the hardest dance to learn'. But her Couple's Choice at Blackpool, to a Destiny's Child medley, holds a special place in her heart.

'That is one of my favourites because of the memories attached to it – getting the first 40 of the series with my mum and my family in the audience. Everything about it was amazing.'

Fleur was thrilled to be able to take her iconic routines on the road, with dance partner Vito, in the *Strictly Come Dancing Live Tour*.

'That was really fun, because I could dance and not worry about leaving the competition,' she says. 'Also, you build up such a strong relationship with your partner, and Vito is literally like a brother to me. Because we weren't learning new dances, we could just be mates and dance.'

Fleur met the cast of the new series at the launch-show rehearsals and says *Strictly* fans are in for a treat.

'There were people that I didn't expect to be able to move as well as they do, so there are going to be some nice surprises,' she says.

Having been in their dancing shoes, Fleur has some sage advice for her successors.

'Enjoy yourself and don't think about it as a competition,' she says. 'That's easier said than done, but when I stopped stressing about getting the dance perfect, and I let go and had fun, it was the best experience ever.'

Now looking forward to her new role, Fleur says she is over the moon to remain part of the *Strictly* family.

'There aren't many people that can say they've been on the show, done the tour and then hosted this show. My journey can continue and doesn't have to end. It's a dream.'

Fleur East

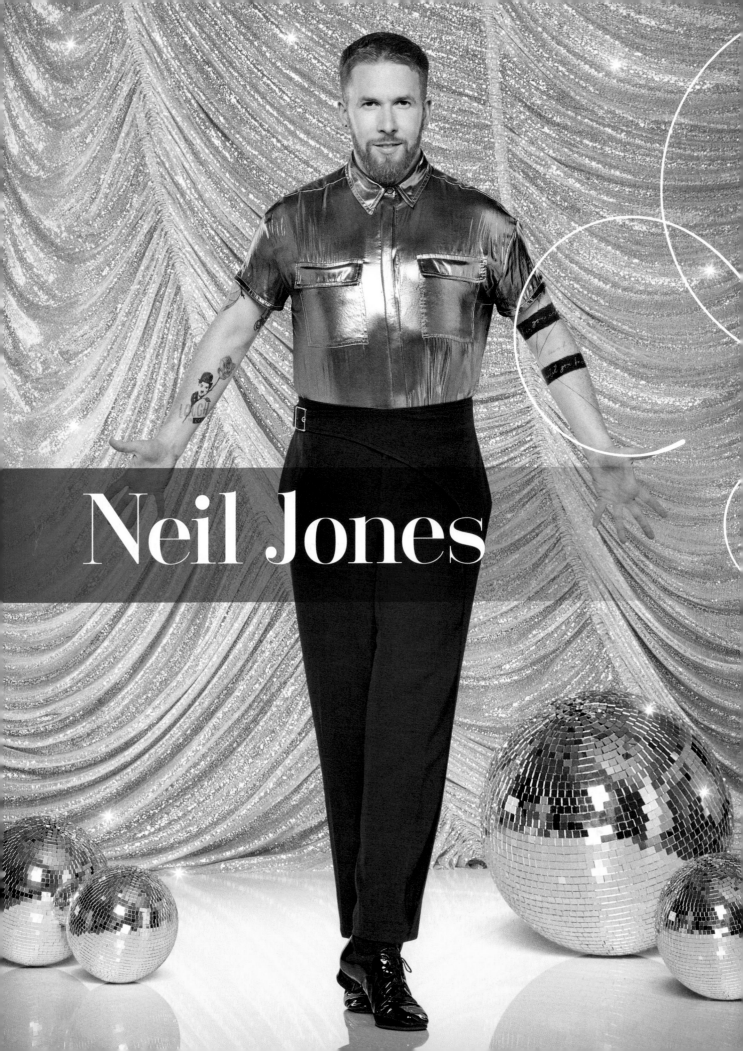

Neil Jones

As one of *Strictly Come Dancing*'s longest-serving pro dancers, Neil is always excited about the start of a new series and says he can't wait to see what this year's celebrities can achieve on the dance floor.

'This series' cast has something for everyone,' he says. 'All the celebrities this year have so much energy. I particularly can't wait to see what they do for their for the Couple's Choice dances.'

With celebrities from all walks of life taking to the *Strictly* ballroom floor, Neil says that other types of dance experience make no difference in the competition.

'It doesn't matter whether you've done other dance forms; learning Latin and ballroom is totally different. It's a whole new ballgame.'

Neil was born in a British army camp in Münster, Germany, and began dancing at three, training in ballet, tap, modern, ballroom and Latin. He has represented Finland, the Netherlands and the UK, and holds 45 dance championship titles, including eight-time British National, eight-time Dutch National, European and four-time World Latin Champion. He joined the pro dance team in 2016 and has previously partnered footballer and broadcaster Alex Scott and comedian Nina Wadia.

As a former World Champion, Neil knows what it takes to become a *Strictly* winner and believes connecting with the viewers is the key.

'It's a word we use a lot, but what makes a *Strictly* champion is definitely the journey,' he says. 'You don't have to be top of the leaderboard every week. You don't even have to get 10s throughout. The most important thing on the show is that connection with the audience.'

Dancing on both the *Strictly Come Dancing Live* tour and the *Strictly: The Professionals* tour this year, Neil says he had a blast with his co-stars.

'We had so much fun and I got to know everyone better and spend more time with the cast, which was great,' he says.

Neil also competed with comedian Rosie Ramsey in the *Strictly* Christmas special and scored an impressive 39 for their seasonal Jive.

'Rosie was a brilliant partner, a great dancer with loads of energy and a massive fan of the show,' he says. 'Teaching her was a dream.'

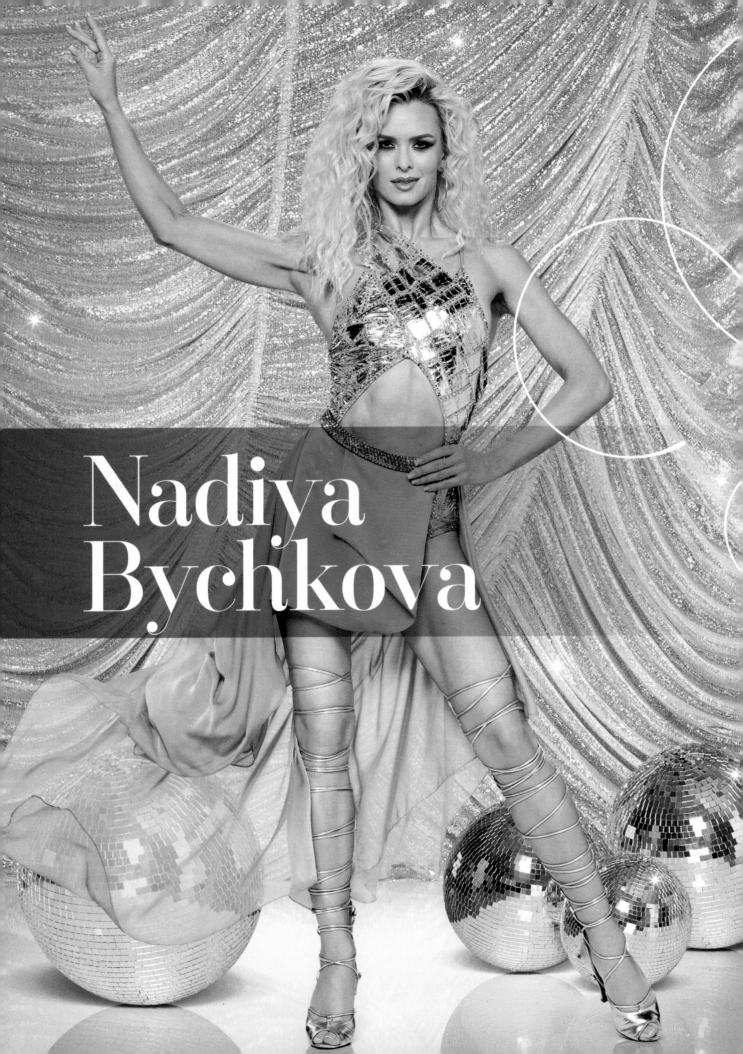

Nadiya Bychkova

Former World Champion Nadiya has seven years of *Strictly Come Dancing* under her sparkly belt and, last year, took to the floor with Bros star Matt Goss. As series 21 kicks off, she says she is impressed by the latest batch of celebrities.

'They are a lovely line-up,' she says. 'There's a beautiful energy between them. There's a lot of talent in the group, so it will be interesting to see where they will take us.'

While the Ukrainian professional dancer is not predicting finalists just yet, she has her own views on what makes a *Strictly* champ.

'A little bit of talent always helps, but also embracing it all and being open to not being perfect, because you're learning,' she says. 'Trust in your partner, because it's such a whirlwind. Once they take that on board, they can buckle up for an incredible ride and might end up with a Glitterball trophy!'

Born in Luhansk, Ukraine, Nadiya was crowned Slovenian Ballroom and Latin Champion multiple times as well as World Champion and European Champion. She joined *Strictly Come Dancing* in 2017. In series 20, she and Matt were eliminated in week four.

'Matt worked hard and listened,' she says. 'He enjoyed learning a new dance every week, learning new movements, new technique, new mechanics.'

Nadiya also had a ball in the Christmas special, dancing with veteran actor Larry Lamb. 'Larry is a legend, a true gent. I remember speaking to his son, George, who told me that to watch his dad dancing on *Strictly*, looking so elegant and happy, was magical. And that's how I felt.'

This year Nadiya promises viewers are in for a treat when it comes to the iconic group numbers, and she says she loved the opening number of the launch show.

'The group dances this year are going to be fabulous, so I'm looking forward to people seeing them. Every year, our Creative Director, Jason Gilkison, makes sure they get better and better. The opening of the show was an incredible production. We filmed the beginning in the Tate Britain and it was beautiful.

'I'm also looking forward to some incredible music acts. It was such a pleasure and honour to dance to Jessie Ware's performance on the launch show. In my first year on *Strictly*, I danced with Davood Ghadami to one of her songs, so it was beautiful to have her performing there.'

As the celebrities take their first steps on the *Strictly* floor, Nadiya has some sound advice.

'Enjoy every moment. Have fun learning new skills. You only get one chance to do it and sometimes you forget [that] because it's such a busy time. It's good to remember that it is an amazing show, which the nation absolutely loves, and to be able to be part of it, to bring that magic to viewers' homes on Saturday and Sunday nights, is just incredible.'

Answers

WORDSEARCH

J	W	O	A	T	I	W	O	J	P	L	Y	X	B	C
F	O	R	T	Y	C	R	A	O	D	G	Y	H	U	J
Z	C	L	E	K	A	R	E	N	H	A	U	E	R	O
C	O	T	M	F	Z	R	P	E	C	O	R	S	L	H
H	D	A	L	U	P	Y	W	S	I	M	D	U	G	A
A	K	S	N	E	S	H	I	R	L	E	Y	Q	J	N
R	H	N	O	O	R	H	C	L	A	U	D	I	A	N
L	D	G	E	K	T	X	T	E	S	M	V	B	L	E
E	C	J	O	H	F	L	E	U	R	E	A	S	T	S
S	P	P	J	Y	Z	T	E	S	K	C	H	A	R	R
T	X	D	U	B	E	K	E	K	N	Z	T	A	W	A
O	E	U	D	F	W	I	P	A	S	L	A	S	Q	D
N	H	I	G	Z	C	H	A	R	D	C	K	B	J	E
N	N	P	E	E	T	E	S	S	D	A	L	Y	L	B
S	C	I	S	G	H	M	D	A	K	K	U	S	H	E

Charleston	Johannes Radebe	Judges	Salsa
Jowita	Claudia	Shirley	Skelton
Forty	Karen Hauer	Fleur East	Jive
Jones	Du Beke	Tess Daly	Mushtuk

CROSSWORD

1 J	A	N	E	T	T	2 E		3 D	4 I	P	5 R	I	M	6 A
						A		7 P		T	O			A
8 J	9 O	E		10 A	N	N	E	K	A		11 B	A	N	D
	D		12 N		G		T		L		E		R	
13 J	U	D	I		14 O	R	E	Y		15 R	Y	A	N	
	D		K			R				T		R		
16 M	U	S	I	C	A	L			17 B	R	I	A	N	
			T						I					
18 S	U	S	A	N				19 A	N	D	R	20 E		
			K			21 K			D			U		
22 L	23 U	L	U		24 M	A	25 M	Y		26 E	M	M	A	
	N		Z		O		T			R		B		
27 A	D	A	M		28 T	A	Y	L	29 O	R		30 J	A	Y
	E		I		S		A		N					
31 F	R	A	N	K	I	E		32 G	E	O	R	G	I	A

QUIZ

1. Adams (Kaye, Jayde, Tony and Nicola). **2.** 'Symphony' by Clean Bandit featuring Zara Larsson. **3.** Karen Hauer. **4.** Jacqui Smith. **5.** Centenary (100 years) of the BBC. **6.** Craig Revel Horwood. **7.** Giovanni Pernice, Graziano Di Prima and Vito Coppola. **8.** Fleur East. **9.** Donny Osmond. **10.** American Smooth. **11.** Kym Marsh. **12.** Darren Gough, Mark Ramprakash and Louis Smith. **13.** Alexandra Mardell. **14.** Ed Balls. **15.** Bill Bailey